THE APAPA SIX:

WEST AFRICA
FROM A
60s
PERSPECTIVE

JOHN BERRYMAN

THE APAPA SIX:
WEST AFRICA FROM A 60s PERSPECTIVE

JOHN BERRYMAN

'The Bahamas: Secondary Social Studies' (3rd Edition, pub 2014).

'The Bible: A Helping Hand' (pub 2002).

'The Church: Defining Moments In Its Western Tradition' (pub 2013).

DEDICATION

Dedicated to SOAS Stakeholders Everywhere, Past, Present and Future, of whom Andrew, Frank, David, Tony and Ian are worthy Ambassadors.

Balboa Press
A Division of Hay House
1663 Liberty Drive
Bloomington, IN 47403
www.balboapress.co.uk
UK TFN: 0800 0148647 (Toll Free inside the UK)
UK Local: 02036 956325 (+44 20 3695 6325 from outside the UK)

ISBN: 978-1-9822-8315-5 (sc)
ISBN: 978-1-9822-8316-2 (e)

Balboa Press rev. date: 04/16/2021

BALBOA.PRESS
A DIVISION OF HAY HOUSE

CONTENTS

PROLOGUE

Has any generation been blessed more abundantly, before or since, than the British baby boomers of the immediate post-war era?: The advent of the Welfare State: the NHS; Council Housing; Secondary Education for All; Full Employment, hence a plethora of job prospects; University expansion, with County Major Awards and State Scholarships to fund Tuition Fees and Accommodation.

That's how it seemed for six of these fortunate products, undergraduates registered at London University's School of Oriental and African Studies, as we submitted our Boarding Passes on the gangway of the Apapa, a vessel of 11,600 tonnage, 479 feet in length, prior to embarking, ex- Liverpool, on a lifechanging experience, the likes of which our parents could have but dreamed. Thus it was, on March 26th 1965 we made due passage, majestically, out of the environs of the Docks to the accompaniment of the receding strains of 'All you need is Love' blasting ashore at the height of Beatlemania as the iconic profile of the domed cathedral-like Port Building receded obstinately from view: each one of us, the products of Middle England, bound for three West African Universities: respectively, Andrew Crozier and Frank Curry scheduled for Ghana at Legon, David Hedges and Ian Piper destined for Ife, and with Tony McWilliams and myself next door at Ibadan in Western Nigeria, courtesy of Elder Dempster Lines, and financially facilitated by virtue of the initiative of Professor Roland Oliver. Tony, with whom I was to share this joint venture over the next few months was a person for whom I had (fortunately) high regard. Of a Christian background like me, a former candidate for the Priesthood, Tony was slight of build, fair-haired and of fair complexion, widely read with a philosophical outlook on life. Inoffensive, quietly spoken, and above all tolerant (mercifully), our companionship would stand the test of time. We could only hope that the intellectual Frank and the academic Andrew; that the dilettante Ian and the serious minded David were to be blessed likewise with mutually good fortune. Such were our pairings. We've all remained friends and kept up with each other ever since; can't have been bad.

School of Oriental and African Studies, University of London

Our application, eighteen months previously, to read History with Special Reference to Africa, at SOAS, had certainly raised a few eyebrows at school from our respective VIth Form UCAS (or UCCA as it was then called) advisers: at the state Grammar Schools in Hastings and Bexhill for example; or in Tony's case from the Monastic Superiors on his decision to retreat from contemplative seminarianism. From the utilitarian vantage point, how would a such an obscure degree at the end of such academic pursuit enhance our future prospects in the context of an increasingly Eurocentric national perspective, as the retreat from our global Empire gathered pace?

Professor Oliver had spearheaded the African History Dept at SOAS in 1960, along with his then dedicated and idealistic colleagues of like vision, D.H. Jones and J.D. Fage; a pioneering trio whose enterprise went such a long way to enhance the study and research in African History across academia worldwide. Within five years the Dept. had more than doubled its staff, with the accession of Richard Gray as Reader, Humphrey Fisher as our academic and pastoral tutor, Shula Marks, Anthony Atmore and distinguished visiting staff such as A. Adu Boahen.

So be it, having enrolled and embraced this novel course, now into our second year and setting off for the experience at first hand. Part of the exchange student package that the course entailed and which Professor Oliver initiated, here was to be for us a term's study at a University in West Africa, plus six weeks or so at the end of it to travel, testing our wits, and interacting at first-hand with the very people who were the focus of our academic pursuit; all of this, a generation prior to the now accepted formality of the likes of the European Erasmus Scheme for example. For its time, such prescience; so life-affirming!

A LIFE ON THE OCEAN WAVE, PART 1

M.V. Apapa: Liverpool to Lagos

Safely stowed: our respective baggage consigned to a small corner of our inside cabin, or 'Stateroom' so called, our 'Tropical Trip', so billed, was under way; familiarising ourselves with the nooks and crannies of our floating hotel; supper in the First Class Dining Room. A full menu at our table for six, of such delights as chilled cantelope, haunch of venison, roast capon, bombed caramel, with selected accompanying wines, was served by a multinational team of waiters dancing attendance. Doubtless this was symptomatic, almost, of the raison d'etre of Elder Dempster, the designated Shipping Line, with its origins in the mid-Nineteenth Century, but trading as such since 1932[1], so familiar to the colonial officials and traders of yesteryear as a ritualistic rite of passage. Douglas Lawson had been one such, the bulk of his career served in the Colonial Service as a Civil Engineer, frequently out in the bush with tent, tools of the trade and personal effects, porterage courtesy of locally recruited personnel. He had been responsible for the supply of a reliable water supply for Kano City and by 1956 he was the designated Head of the Public Works Department answerable directly to the Governor of Nigeria. The Elder Dempster experience has been related to me by his daughter, Angela, who later became the effective facilitator of all things non-academic at Bede's School in Sussex where I subsequently taught, and a water-colour painter of some note. Angela had by then married Roger Perrin, the school's founding Headmaster, who employed me, and for whom I shall be forever grateful: small world; we've become good family friends, but not until 40 years later did we make the connexion. Roger's account in his book, recounting the tentative genesis of this successful boarding school, is a true story of a partnership in itself; with Angela, and as initiated by Peter Pyemont. It's recommended reading for all who contemplate a career in teaching or educational management.[2].

So, here were we, rubbing shoulders on board with a few residual expatriate functionaries, effectively experiencing the tail end of an era: an era such as had been mapped out, politically and quite literally, at the Berlin Conference as convened on November 15th, 1884. For the ensuing three months diplomats representing the interests of European nations had gathered round a horseshoe shaped table in the official residence on Wilhelmstrasse of Count Otto von Bismarck, Germany's Imperial Chancellor at whose behest the conference had been summoned. With a huge wall map of the African continent pinned to the wall, 'drooping down like a question mark', according to Prof. Godfrey Uzoigwe[3], staring the likes of Alphonse de Courcel of France, the Portuguese Antonio Jose de Serra Gomes, Edward Malet from Britain and Belgium's Gabriel August van der Straten in the face. The ostensible purpose of this high-powered meeting was to resolve matters in dispute relating to King Leopold II of Belgium's dubious business activity in the Congo Basin, and as such provoking reaction from Portugal who had longstanding claims in the region[4]. Inevitably all other interested parties were drawn in, not least Bismarck's concern that with other European states wanting to muscle in on the rich pickings which Africa had to offer, Germany's role as a world power could be compromised and that its 'rightful place in the sun' would be denied unless he showed his mettle by taking the initiative. Around the table, the absence of any direct African representation was palpable. The outcome of these negotiations was ratified by February 26th 1885, with the signing of the 'Berlin Treaty'. This diplomatic conclusion, as prompted by Germany's Iron Chancellor, in the wider context, was all about access to markets, and competing European spheres of influence in a continent whose internal mysteries were being explored, uncovered, and whose natural resources exploited yet further: the imperative of 'The Dual Mandate', as Lord Lugard was later, euphemistically, to coin it.[5], Less euphemistically, Nijman, Muller, and de Blij, are straight to the point: 'The Berlin Conference was Africa's undoing in more ways than one … a legacy of political pragmatism that could neither be eliminated or made to operate satisfactorily'[6]. Its repercussions have significant resonance in today's world.

West Africa, 1965. Seaward Outward and Inward Itinerary of the
Apapa Six, 1965. (Graphics courtesy of Anouk Berryman)

Scheduled to call in at the four anomalous West African territories, formerly British Colonial Protectorates, now independent Nations, we were destined to witness at first hand the direct consequences of the mercenary decisions taken by those European diplomats assembled in the capital of Bismarck's Germany back then. Spheres of influence on the continent of Africa were delineated at this, as it was to turn out, defining conference to protect respective European national 'trading and strategic interests': scant, if any, regard paid to sensitivities and values of the hapless indigenous inhabitants, even by the standards of Gladstone's sceptical Liberal Ministry in the U.K. From this vague statement of principles evolved the assertion of Imperial sovereignty over pretty much the entire African continent by the 'fin de siecle'; internationally recognised frontiers drawn up arbitrarily in the name of the respective metropolitan powers.[7] Hence, our ports of call in 1965 were predetermined inevitably at the four amorphous Anglocentric entities en route: The Gambia, Sierra Leone, Ghana and Nigeria: a voyage in excess of 5,000 miles spanning a cruise of nearly two weeks; a voyage in the wake of Bartholemew Diaz whose less than speedy and questionably salubrious pioneering seafaring venture of coastal discovery as he nosed his Portuguese fleet of sailing vessels tentatively down the West Coast finally reaching the continent's southern extremity by rounding the Cape, back in 1487. A voyage, too, in the shadow of those European sailing vessels on the first leg of the 'Triangular Trade', laden at this stage with metropolitan 'goodies': textiles, firearms, manufactured goods, cowrie shells, glass beads, destined for the delectation of indigenous African potentates, in exchange for human merchandise, whose enforced captivity was characterised by the trans-Atlantic 'Middle Passage' chains. The 'cargo' would then be exchanged for the products at the ports of the USA and Caribbean, for products of the New World, cotton, tobacco, sugar, as conveyed on the last leg of the journey back to the ship's home port.

The infamous Bay of Biscay greeted us, true to form, as we awoke from our slumber first night: the contents of our previous evening's meal was regurgitated periodically during the course of Saturday morning, as the valiant vessel ploughed its way regardless through the unrelenting mountainous waves. The distribution of sea sickness tablets by the ship's doctor brought some relief by the next day, a Sunday, when calmer waters associated with the Canary Islands, as sited in the distance, played their part decisively in allaying the discomforture which had so blighted our initial southward venture. Subsequently, as the blue skies presaged the more settled ambience, the trip followed the normal pattern familiar to aficionados of the cruise culture: Table Tennis, Deck Quoits, Fitness Facilities, Desk Strolling, Browsing in the well stocked Library during the day; live entertainment, Recorded Recitals, Bingo, Bridge Tournaments, Whist Drives, 'Dog Racing', Cinema featuring 'Bedtime Story' with Marlon Brando and David Niven after supper. Wednesday was Carnival Night; a supper extravaganza with all the trimmings, and Party atmosphere mandatory. The Fare again pretentious and inscrutable by our lower middle class standards, we were served up with such delicacies as 'Veloute Irma',' Vol au Vent Laguipierre', 'Kangaroo Tail Soup', 'Franzipan Slices', 'Angels on Horseback'. That's what the Menu proclaimed, anyway, followed by singing, dancing, and cigars smoked with too much gusto for my own good. The coast of Africa was clearly within our line of vision by Thursday. Our sense of anticipation was generated by the prospect of setting foot for the first time the following day on the continent, the history of which was the chosen focus of our undergraduate specialisation.

The Apapa Six Party Time aboard M.V. Apapa, 31ˢᵗ March 1965. Clockwise, L to R Frank Curry, Ian Piper, The Writer, Tony McWilliams, David Hedges, Andrew Crozier

Deck Tennis Final: Tony in the Blue Shirt

So it was: on Friday 2nd April the 'Apapa' veered West and on up the River Gambia Estuary, from which The Gambia nation itself takes its name (not the other way round), towards the port and capital city . Bathurst (now Banjul), on the river estuary's southern bank, loomed ever closer. By 5:45 p.m. we were on the wharf, surrounded by an inquisitive meleé of humanity comprising a variety of vendors pressing hard upon us to purchase their wares ranging from goatskin handbags to dyed headdresses and peanuts; and there were the little kids with nothing to offer except to serve as walking tour guides around the metropolis. As I engaged one, Omar Secka, a young Wolof Muslim lad aged about eight years, taking him up on his offer, and ingested the tropical atmosphere for the first time, I could only muse at this Lilliputian, inscrutable country which was his birthright; the alleged homeland of Kunta Kinte, hero of Alex Haley's acclaimed novel 'Roots'[8]: realistically, the quintessential outcome of that fateful Berlin conference eighty years before.

We arrived just two months since the formal granting of its Independence back in February. This sliver of territory, a little finger thrust into the heart of francophone Senegal, is defined by the river from which it takes its name. Its population, very largely of Islamic provenance, is made up of three main ethnic groupings: the Wolof, largely Islamised, who claim descent from the ancient Empire of Mali, the Malinke whose ancestry is strongly derivative of the medieval Songhai Empire of the Upper Niger, and the Fulani, Islamic pastoralists from inland Futa Toro, in the semi-desert region astride the middle Senegal River. As with much of the Forest Rainbelt of West Africa, the region had been blighted by the demands of the iniquitous Trans-Atlantic Slave Trade throughout the sixteenth to nineteenth centuries. Until, that is Great Britain, for commercial as well as humanitarian reasons, unilaterally, at first, abolished it in 1807. Determined to enforce the law outlawing this now illicit trade, St. Mary's Island on which Banjul stands was purchased from the local 'Chief' by the British in 1816 as a Royal Naval Base to deter contravention of the 1807 legislation. Thus trade and infrastructure links evolved in the light of this contact, and the significantly navigable river provided a valuable conduit for commercial arrangements with local groupings inland in such products as animal hides and importantly, groundnuts. Competition amongst these local indigenous 'kingdoms' proved fatal to the long term autonomy of these little states, as the French began to muscle in on the lucrative West African trade emanating from their own tentative contacts in neighbouring Senegal, as the nineteenth century unfolded[9]. That's where, again, the aforementioned Berlin Conference played a defining role. It had paved the way for a Franco/British Treaty in 1889, which formally acknowledged effective control of Senegal by the French, with a concession of exclusive rights to the U.K. based on the Gambia River, to a limit of 300 miles upstream from the Atlantic Coast and with a 30 mile or so 'hinterland' straddling the conduit to the north and south[10].

Bathurst Cityscape 1965

First Day in Africa: The Writer outside Bathurst Post Office, April 2nd 1965

My couple of hours with Omar were revealing. With great pride he took me along the main waterfront with its official designated mansions: Government House, residence of the Governor-General, Sir John Paul, with his uniformed guards on parade in their khaki uniforms and red kaftan caps; the Prime Minister, Alhaji Sir Dawda Jawara's official pad, close by: each situated so as to take full advantage of the cooling off-shore Atlantic breezes, with a bevvy of official Mercedes saloons at the beck and call of Ministers of State plying the treelined boulevard. Contrast this to the next stage of my guided tour: that of the abode of the average citizen, barely a few hundred yards away, but shielded from the view of the political elite: a conglomeration of shanties, cheek by jowl, a place that Omar himself called home. Domestic 'Facilities', toilets, ovens and the like, all outside, were the norm; mud encrusted alleyways, one or two locally owned stores, where I purchased a couple of bottles of Pepsi to share with Omar, in the process passing a European Catholic Priest exercising his vocation, presumably calling in to give succour to what seemed to be his benighted flock. Then it was back to the vessel for an 8 p.m. departure, bidding a fond farewell and a proffered 'gratuity' for Omar with whom I subsequently stayed in contact for a few years. What this initiation into the African experience had already taught me, along with my five friends, each of whom had opted to explore the city on his own, was the sheer inequity the colonial experience had wrought upon Africa: the indiscriminate splitting of formerly cohesive tribal groupings, now alienated by virtue of being on different sides of the artificially constructed national frontier, for metropolitan convenience; secondly, the sheer inequity of a system that had acquiesced, some would say encouraged, the widening material gap between the privileged few and the dispossessed many; thirdly, the influence of Islam, and for that matter, Christianity, which had become so pervasive in African culture and which, perversely, were to sow further seeds of mutual disaffection most notably in Nigeria as we shall see.[11] Back on board ship, with our separate tales to relate, whilst contemplating our customary evening meal, we were astounded to encounter on the main deck a host of a hundred or so 'deck passengers', accompanied by their limited possessions and shielded by a crudely all-embracing tarpaulin, seeking better fortune elsewhere along the coast as the 'Apapa' eased its way out of its temporary berth to expedite our progress for the next few days; they, condemned to their makeshift accommodation; we, by the vehicle of our pampered western expectations.

A day at sea ensued en route for Freetown, most of it spent lounging on top deck reading, but nevertheless conscious of our fellow travellers, the Deck Passengers, struggling for a mere tolerable existence several feet below us, with only their improvised tarpaulin as protection from the relentless daytime tropical heat. The evening was rounded off on board, with the six of us congregated around the Monopoly board in the 'Smoking Room': our confirmed ultra lefty, and Secretary of London University Student Union's Socialist Society, Ian, brazenly wiped the rest of us clean, with hotels on Mayfair, Park Lane, and even charging us rent when one or other of us, having just collected our £200 for passing Go, had the temerity to land on Old Kent Road; no shame, no mercy, or perhaps just an exercise in virtual 'Know your Enemy'.

Sunday Morning, early, saw us docking at the Queen Elizabeth II Wharf in the aptly named capital, Freetown; its nomenclature evocative all that Sierra Leone represents in the course of West Africa's turbulent history. As Fourah Bay College, the first Western University on the west coast, founded in 1827, looked down imperiously upon us from Mount Aureol ('Serra Lyoa': the Hill of the Lion, so called by the early Portuguese voyagers) to our left, we pondered the mixed fortunes influencing the nation's story as it had edged towards its Independence in 1961. In many ways the small nation represents the full gamut of Britain's association with the west coast. With its natural deep-water harbour, and a secluded fortified island upstream, Bunce Island had for long been a prime site for striking lucrative deals in human trafficking. Here John Newton had been operative; ex-naval man, raffish, bully, blasphemer, womaniser, drunkard, he kind of fitted in with the sort of enterprise as befitted the notorious activities on the island. Even by its own dubious standards, Newton was so detestable, he was himself forced into servitude to a high-ranking woman of the indigenous Sherbro people, one Princess Peye; effectively, he was a white slave, treated as any other. That is, until he was rescued at the behest of his father in 1750. For two more years he served on three trans-Atlantic slaving voyages before the recollection of a near death experience convinced him of the error of his previous life-style. In 1754 he gave up his rakish existence, convinced that the Lord had saved him for a purpose. He initially took up bureaucratic employment in Liverpool, candidated, and was accepted, into Holy Orders, becoming Vicar of Olney, in Buckinghamshire. Here he lavished care on the poor and destitute, urged William Wilberforce to persevere with his Anti-Slave-Trade Bill in Parliament and co-operated with William Cowper in writing a collection of sacred hymns. Among these are, of course, 'How sweet the name of Jesus sounds', and 'Amazing Grace'. He died rejoicing the knowledge that Wilberforce's Bill had just been passed the Commons in 1807.[12] In many ways the fortunes of this man mirror the dealings of Great Britain with its colony of Sierra Leone: from abhorrent bestiality to philanthropic humanity.

Freetown's incarnation in the eighteenth century, its 'raison d'etre', was to provide a permanent settlement for erstwhile slaves thus effectively freed in Great Britain on the back of Lord Mansfield's Judgement of 1772. The case, brought before King's Bench by the British abolitionist Granville Sharp on behalf of a runaway slave, one James Somerset, highlighted the plight of the 'black poor', those having been 'liberated', but now rootless in the big cities with no means of support. Furthermore, many of the slaves who had 'earned' their freedom by fighting for the British during the War of American Independence had originally been settled in Nova Scotia, and had become disillusioned there: segregation, and the climate didn't help. These 'Black Loyalists' certainly had a case.

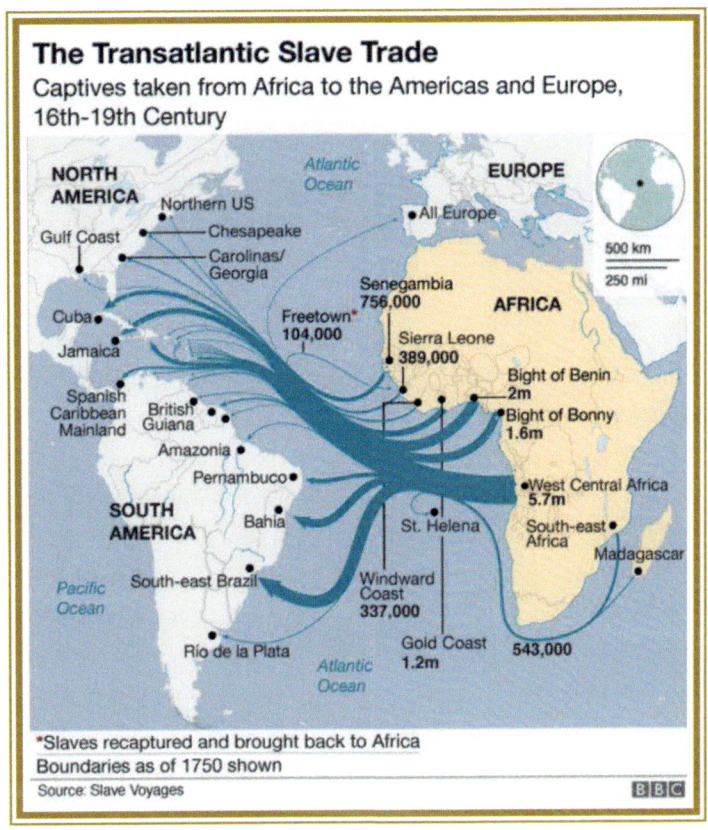

Slave Woman pounding cassava, Jamaica, c 1810: William Berryman; watercolour, sketch.

The advocacy of ethnic 'civil rights' coinciding with the evolution of educated articulate Africans, was emerging in London, empowered in part by the Mansfield Judgement: The 'Sons of Africa'. Prominent among this forward thinking group was Olaudah Equiano, whose role in the abolition movement has for too long been understated. A former slave himself, by his own account, having been captured as a seven year old Igbo, around 1750, in the West African Benin 'Empire' in what is today the nation state of Nigeria, his experience being subsequently sold from pillar to post in the Caribbean and North America became the stuff of legend. By a stroke of good fortune, a benign slave owner facilitated the wherewithal to purchase his freedom in 1766 for the princely sum of £40, He resorted to England, served as a crewman on various voyages of discovery, became not only merchant, but a master of literacy, having converted to Christianity. He joined the 'Sons of Africa' in 1773, gaining the ear of Granville Sharp and William Wilberforce in his quest to ameliorate the plight of his fellow ethnics. His graphic description of the Zong Massacre of 1781, whereby the vast bulk of slaves on board the trans-Atlantic slaver (the 'Zong') were dumped into the sea when the supply of drinking water was diminishing, added fuel to the crusade. This was given a shot in the arm by the publication in 1789 of his autobiography. 'The Interesting Narrative of the Life of Olaudah Equiano'. This for its time became a best seller, a personal chronicle detailing for public consumption the sheer inhumanity of what the individual slave was perforce to endure. Also known by a 'given' name, Gustavus Vasa, which he resented, Equiano finally settled in London in 1792, marrying a white woman, Susannah Cullen, by whom he had two daughters, dying in 1797 at the age of 52. It is often argued that Equiano was the Martin Luther King of his day, such was his contemporary profile. The journal hit hard, and its literary influence could be regarded almost on par with Harriet Beecher Stowe's 'Uncle Tom's Cabin' with its impression on Abraham Lincoln in the U.S.A. during the 1850s, in the run-up to the Civil War.

Ever a man to put his idealism into practice, Sharp insisted such a testimony should be rewarded, as was the patriotism of the aforementioned 'Black Loyalists' in Nova Scotia, ideally by seeking to 'repatriate' its people to the 'motherland'. In the name of the 'Committee for the relief of the Black Poor', Sharp duly negotiated the 'purchase' in 1787, of some West African 'real estate', down river from Bunce Island, courtesy of 'King Tom' a Koya Temne 'Chief'. This site was destined, hopefully, to become the nucleus for which freed slaves could settle in 'perpetuity'. Uncertainty characterised the legality as to what the terms of this contract of purchase actually entailed, and 'Granville Town' (also known as Cline Town) was subject to constant harassment from neighbouring tribesmen. Inadequate supplies, starvation, disease wracked the infant colony, to the point whereby some of its settlers themselves turned to the lucrative enterprise in human trafficking based at the entrepôt on Bunce Island, ironically as we have seen, a British possession, 18 miles or so up the Sierra Leone River.[13] Notable amongst these was a certain James de Mane, a former slave himself whom Sharp had a hand in personally rescuing.[14] Following much acrimony, 'King Jimmy', King Tom's successor, released the infant settlement of its misery by putting the village to the torch. There could be no security until a more practical commitment was forthcoming from the British. Lieut. John Clarkson, brother of abolitionist Thomas Clarkson sought out a fresh locale in 1792 nearby, at which point the settlement reinvented itself as Freetown. More settlers joined the initial intake and despite similar privations the colony survived. Lessons had been learned. Ideally situated, the colony served as the de facto capital for all Britain's West African coastal possessions, as well as serving as the naval H.Q. of the British West Africa Squadron from 1808 to 1874 in its efforts to stamp out and intercept illicit Slave Trading in the Atlantic after Britain itself had outlawed the trade in 1807. The Kings's Arch in Freetown, now forming the gateway to the Government Hospital, was erected as a testimonial to this endeavour, its inscription plate originally proclaiming that 'Any slave who passes through this gate is a free man'. The venerable Cotton Tree which we observed adjacent to the present Supreme Court Building is said to be the arboreal symbol under the shades of which those first Nova Scotian settlers offered prayers of thanksgiving on first setting foot in their 'promised land' in 1792. As such it remains the symbol of Sierra Leone and all that it stands for. In many ways, Sierra Leone represents the essence of British activities in West Africa. The fortress at Bunce Island had been the hub of the market for trade in human commerce, sadly contributing to Britain's contribution as the largest dealer in trans-Atlantic slaves at the height of the iniquitous enterprise[15]. Yet, using Sierra Leone as the base for its operations, it became the focal point of Britain's determination to eradicate such trade; paradoxically, the first European nation state in fact to do so. At least Granville Town and Freetown are testimonies to this philanthropic initiative, as the following account illustrates.

That's where the story of the Rev. Samuel Ajayi Crowther is instructive here, very much in the tradition of Equiano referred to earlier, adding further illustrative colour to the West African panorama of the nineteenth century. As a 12 year old illiterate Yoruba lad living in Osogun Village, now in Western Nigeria, Ajayi and his family were abducted in 1821 by Fulani slavers, and sold to Portuguese agents in Lagos for transportation to America. While still in port the Portuguese vessel was intercepted by the British Naval Squadron. Following an armed confrontation and submission of the errant slaver, the potential victims, including Ajayi, were freed and ultimately relocated to Freetown, the haven for liberated slaves. Here the young boy took advantage of any education on offer, and was the very first student to enrol at the newly founded Church Missionary Society's Fourah Bay College in 1827. Quick to learn, with a vast reservoir of intelligence, Ajayi became a scholar in the Classics, African Languages and Theology pursuing further studies in the U.K. Ordained as an Anglican priest, he became the first black Bishop in the Anglican Communion, as marked by due ceremony at Canterbury Cathedral in 1864. His subsequent return to his own homeland, in what would become Nigeria, is the stuff of legend. Now Bishop of the Niger Diocese, his scholarship turned to translating the Bible into his native Yoruba tongue, and he compiled a lexicon of the Hausa language. In this he had collaborated with Rev Owen Emeric Vidall, an Englishman ordained as the first Bishop of Sierra Leone in 1852, in the post of which he served until his untimely death from fever at sea in 1855. This has resonance with my own association as a subsequent teacher at Bede's School in the Sussex village of Upper Dicker, where a friend of mine, Rev. Simon Morgan, was for several years Priest-in Charge of the Parish Church of Holy Trinity, which still serves as the school's Chapel. This Parish had been Vidall's own previous incumbency from 1843 to 1854, prior to his elevation to the episcopacy, and where a tribute to his memory is to be found. Bishop Crowther's time in England was hailed, his public lectures around the country being oversubscribed, feted by the University of Oxford, and granted an audience with Queen Victoria at her request. He retired to Lagos, where he passed away in 1891, by a strange twist of fortune, within shouting distance of his having been set at liberty all those years before: an even more meaningful liberty now. I think this personal story illustrates by analogy the essence of the African experience in the nineteenth century. It's all there: traditional tribal culture, disturbed by the demands of a pernicious slaving commerce, alleviated by a Christian practical conscience as evidenced from the burgeoning Missionary work, thereby facilitating the potential leadership of the indigenous African into the ambience and equal interaction with the wider world.[16] It's symptomatic of the evolution of 'Kingdom People', as documented in David Bown's account of his own ministry in a hitherto marginalised community.[17]

Nevertheless, at the time, the freed slave element in the Freetown colony (the 'Creoles') were destined to be outnumbered by settlers emanating from the interior of Sierra Leone, and a cosmopolitan community evolved in the growing city throughout the nineteenth century. The British actively encouraged legitimate trade with the tribal elders in the hinterland to compensate for their material loss incurred by the abolition of the Slave Trade. Palm Oil, Cocoa, Coffee, Palm Kernels were all sought after tropical goods for the British market; their development was encouraged as 'legitimate trade'. As ever there was the danger of the French and Portuguese encroaching upon what was felt to be British commercial interests. Again, therefore, the decisions taken at the Berlin Conference led to the British annexation of Temne chieftainships to the north of the city, and Mende fiefdoms to its south. 'Protectorate' status was thus imposed on the hinterland and British sovereignty asserted: in effect a pre-emptive strike. The terminology and practice was carefully chosen, for a parsimonious treasury back home was ever keen to limit administrative costs. As will be seen the subsequent colonial philosophy of Lord Lugard, he of the 'Dual Mandate', was to come up with an acceptable resolution in the guise of 'Indirect Rule' as a resolution to this Imperial conundrum.[18]

The Cotton Tree, Freetown

Memorial to Owen Vidall , Parish Church
of Holy Trinity, Upper Dicker

The King's Gate, Freetown

Tony and I strolled round the central section of Freetown. Being Sunday, most stores and shops were closed, while the Churches appeared well patronised. Indeed as we passed by the Anglican Cathedral we were aware of its being broadcast nationally on the state radio station; from the street, a stereophonic effect. Muslims, outnumbering Christians by 3 to nationally, in their distinctive native dress, were content to open up their little convenience shops in the run-down areas of the city. At one of these, barely the size of a wardrobe, we purchased a Coca Cola to share between us, in recognition of our trawl through the insanitary sameness of small shacks and existing a stone's throw from the wealthy business and administrative centre. On our return to the dock we were reminded of the vital role played by Freetown in the two World Wars: a revictualing port for the Atlantic Fleet, and a centre for anti-U boat operations: Freetown once again living up to its name. At least for some.

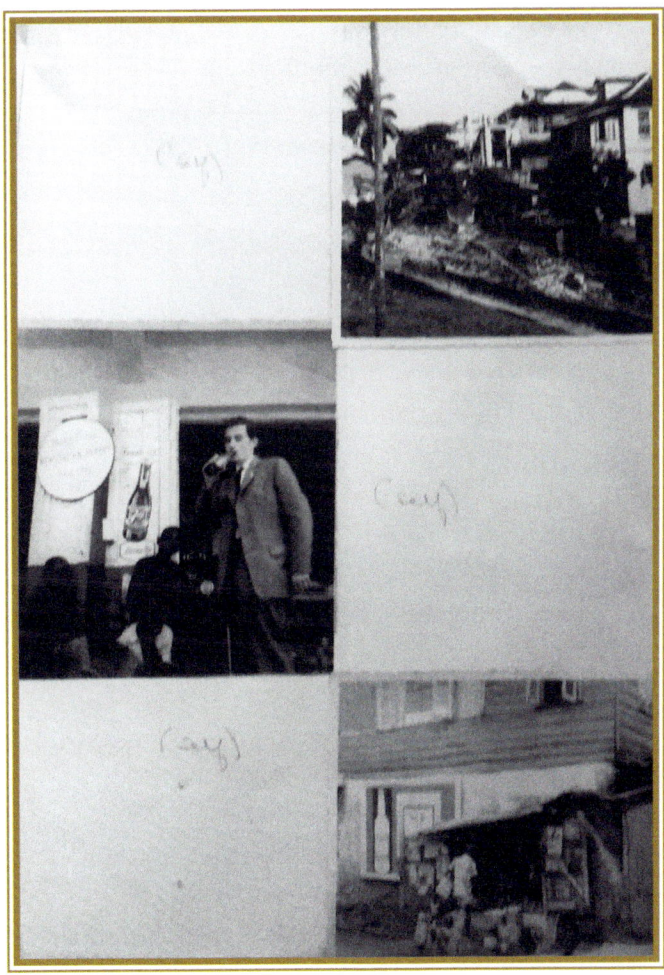

A Stroll Around Freetown

Back to the vessel then: two days at sea without landfall, but with the coasts of Liberia and Cote d'Ivoire to our nautical port, with natural entertainment furnished in the expansive Atlantic to starboard. Sharks and Dolphins made sea sport as they surfaced playfully; a barely disguised seduction ruse for us to join them. My preference, unsurprisingly, was to opt for more familiar territory, as I teamed up with the Passengers XI in the deck cricket 'Test Match' against a team carefully selected from the Crew. Nets duly improvised, strategically placed so as to avoid the fielders having to retrieve the ball from the bottom of the sea, a good natured contest ensued. Honest and good sportsmanship prevailed as my five companions willed us on from the 'Stands' on the Bridge. An opportunity was missed, I felt, by failing to consider representation from our 'Deck Passengers' as a gesture of solidarity and inclusivity, but it wasn't to be. Colonial attitudes die hard. My recollection of the details of the match, and the finer analysis of strategy employed, elude me after the passage of time; save, that is, for the all important result: Passengers' victory by 39 runs; not to mention my own contribution, a batting score of 12, and a haul of 2 wickets. Celebratory drinks to follow, and an evening at the cinema, where a showing of 'The Chalk Garden' filmed in and around Eastbourne brought with it some wistful yearnings for home. Next day ushered heavy rain in the morning, followed by a sultry soporific afternoon as we anticipated our arrival in Tema on the Wednesday, and our farewells to Andrew and Frank where they were to disembark to take up their place at the University of Ghana's campus based in Legon, close by Accra.

Tema a modern port constructed in the 1950s, to handle its burgeoning international trade in Cacao, primarily, conveniently located some 18 miles east of Ghana's capital, Accra, at around 7 a.m., saw roughly half of our fellow Deck Passengers disgorged onto the wharf with scant formality. Andrew and Frank were summoned to the Border and Customs Office where they were duly whisked off to Legon in a University car. It was to be a couple of months or so before we saw them again. The remaining four of us were invited to join a Ghanaian sponsored tour of Accra and its environs by minibus, which we duly accepted.

Ghanaian Stool, Traditional Symbol of the Authority of the Asantahene. (Image courtesy of Livingston Berryman)

This was Ghana, formerly the Gold Coast, showcase and model, as the first tropical country in sub Saharan Africa to have achieved its Independence, under the charismatic Kwame Nkrumah in 1957. The very name of the country resonated with the name of a former medieval empire way to the North, then straddling the River Niger, enriched by its control of the lucrative Trans Saharan Trade in gold and salt: a land, then, of legendary peace and prosperity.[19] Initially impressed by the absence of poverty which had so characterised our impressions of Banjul and Freetown, it became apparent that our tour was edited and orchestrated in order to impress the visitors with the wisdom of Solomon as incarnated in Nkrumah's personality cult as 'Osagyefo the President'. The inspiring edifices to reflect his genius included the prestigious 'Black Star Gate' the entreé into 'Black Star Square' where the 'Black Star National Soccer Team' was being feted ... basically 'Black Star This', 'Black Star That', in deference to the late, enigmatic Marcus Garvey, incorporating the saner visions of Martin Luther King and W.E. du Bois, in whose tradition Nkrumah felt he rightfully belonged. The recently constructed Flagstaff House, built in the style of the 'Golden Stool', symbol of the influential Asantehene, Kingship of Ashanti, was now the President's official residence befitting his messianic status. So appropriate this, as the Ashanti Empire of the Akan tribal grouping under Osei Tutu had frustrated British interior expansion and formal occupation throughout the nineteenth century, even after the Berlin Conference; this by Tutu's judicious exploitation of the gold, and timber resources as 'tools of the trade', in the rainforest and savannah region' just to the north'. That is, until military capitulation was sustained in the Ashanti capital, Kumasi, at the appropriately named Battle of the Golden Stool in 1900. It was the Ashanti, too, who had stood steadfastly in the way of the nineteenth century Muslim Fulani expansion from the North, whose presence in neighbouring Nigeria was to prove a significant factor in its national development.[20] Hence, unusually for West Africa, Christianity has remained the religion of choice for most Ghanaians, with Islamic adherence barely exceeding 20%, and pre-colonial religious beliefs even fewer.

Independence Arch, leading to Black Star Square, Accra

So, after a lite bite at the well appointed Ambassador Hotel, the four of us took ourselves off for an hour's stroll at our leisure to savour the bustling central market; again relatively well organised with all and sundry items for sale as befitted this national showpiece. Then it was back to the minibus, with a brief stop at the entrance to the imposing Legon campus of the University to which Frank and Andrew had been assigned. One little story associated with Legon sprang to mind. A distinguished Lecturer, a man for whose intellect and integrity I had and still have high regard, Dr. (later Professor at Warwick) Jack Scarisbrick, who taught us the European content of our course at Queen Mary College, had done a stint teaching at the University of Ghana at Legon. At the end of his contract, he instructed his steward to pack his personal effects "very carefully, no breakages, no mishaps, mind!": china, cutlery, clothes and the like, ready for his departure. That done to his satisfaction, Jack instructed the compliant steward to leave the baggage thus packed in the room. "This stuff is now all yours, and thank you for your services", or words to that effect, was Jack's parting shot, leaving a very happy colleague gobsmacked by such a generous spirit. That story was relayed to me by a mutual friend, Dr. Kevin MacDonnell also of Queen Mary College. I'd like to think it to be true, for it expresses the essence of Jack and his world view. After Legon, then, our minibus driver deposited us with due formality back to the Dock. During our absence, a Soviet trading vessel had berthed alongside, its crew craning its collective neck as it reflected on the self-evidential inequity exuded by the 'Apapa': 'Deck Passengers' segregated from 'First Class' ; an implicit signal that Russian Cold War diplomacy was determined to muscle in on the political vacuum left by the departing Imperialists. Our own priority was to return to our Stateroom, gather up our assorted belongings from the ship's hold, secure them. Next day we'd be in Lagos, or more technically the port of Apapa, the accredited passenger terminal, our fore-ordained point of disembarkation and from which our motor vessel had presumably been named.

Federal Parliament Building: fronted by statue of Queen Elizabeth II, Lagos

This, then, was Lagos in prospect, the then enigmatic capital of Nigeria, situated incongruously at the South Western extremity of the most densely populated nation in Africa, land mass area of some 350, 000 square miles, home to some 150 million people with 250 indigenous languages spoken or more; randomly thrown and cobbled together at the whim of nineteenth century imperial presumption. As per the bulk of the West African coast already noted, the European toeholds on terra firma which were to be the springboard of subsequent European occupation, were originally the products of the fifteenth century Portuguese, of Renaissance inspired exploratory initiative. Records show that as early as 1472 they had established the genesis of occupation on the Bight of Benin at a suitably protected harbour complex of four islands within a stone's throw of the mainland: Lagos, its choice of name itself betraying its origins. Already occupied by a Yoruba fishing community, subject nominally to the contemporary Benin empire[21], the base evolved into a Portuguese trading emporium,[21a] sadly, as per usual, with trans-Atlantic 'interests' at its heart. With the rise of British involvement in the region, much later, throughout the nineteenth century, the importance of the acquisition of the port increased as its more acceptable commercial contacts in the interior demanded a secure outlet as an ocean-going conduit; defining moment in the aforementioned saga of Samuel Ajayi Crowther for a start. Furthermore, as with Freetown and Bathurst, it provided a base for the naval interception of illicit Atlantic slaving vessels during the Victorian era. Accordingly, by 'local arrangement', Lagos was transferred to overt British control in 1861, initially co-ordinated as one arm of the British West African mini settlements on the coast. Interest had already been stimulated by the exploration into the interior by way of the Niger River such as that mounted by the Scotsman Mungo Park in his attempt to track down the source of the legendary waterway in the early 1800s. This, and for that matter, John Hanning Speke's forays into East Africa, not to mention the much vaunted Livingstone and Stanley episode, had motivated the initiative of enterprising business opportunities. Foremost in the region, among these, was Sir George Goldie's Royal Niger Company, as chartered, date significant, in 1886, whose amalgamation and monopoly of British commercial interests saw off domestic and foreign competition; in the process, the Company turned to putting its resources into a quasi-administration of Southern Nigeria, as the area was later to become: echoes of the East India Co. and the contemporary British South Africa Company of Cecil Rhodes.[22]

This was given philosophical justification in the guise of Lord Lugard's articulation penned (1922) as his 'Dual Mandate': to further the 'economic benefits for the metropole' as well as for enhancing the well-being of indigenous populations with the benefits and privileges of implicit British paternalism; basically seizing the inspired British imperative to expose the riches of Africa to the wider world, while at the same time to share with the indigenous populous some of the benefits and practices of European civilisation.[23] Ever more venturous, Goldie headed north, to check French ambitions, and signed 'treaties' with the Islamic Emirs of Sokoto and Gondo, gaining controlling interest in the Benue River hinterland. By 1899, a more definitive British administration was perceived as imperative, as specialised administrative skills were not the prime focus of the Company. Joseph Chamberlain, Lord Salisbury's ambitious Colonial Secretary, took it on, but with reluctance to spend British taxpayers' money. Take a bow, Frederick Lugard: his 'Indirect Rule' policy was an ideal solution. Guarantee the position, rights, customs of these Islamic potentates in the North, with a formalised hierarchical structure of their own, in return for which a British Protectorate would be acknowledged over the huge swathe now to be known as Northern Nigeria, with Lugard first as High Commissioner (1900-06) and then as Governor (1912-14). Simultaneously Lugard was appointed Governor of the Protectorate of Southern Nigeria in 1900, the British Government having assumed direct oversight of its governance, and to which the Lagos Colony was annexed in 1906. Might as well consolidate the whole, then, opined Lugard, and in 1914, the two Protectorates were merged as 'One Nigeria'; as it turned out, more for administrative convenience rather than as a sop to indigenous sensitivities.[24] The shadow of 'Berlin' brooded incessantly, with even greater irony, given the year: Sarajevo and all that!

Northern Nigeria itself had inherited the legacy of militant Islam, its religion and culture infused and absorbed into the Hausa population dominant in the region by the start of the nineteenth century. Islam, like Christianity, had advanced far and away from its cradleland. For Christianity it had been the road and sea links as sponsored by the Roman Empire which had made possible the missionary journeys of Paul, the Apostle to the Gentiles. For Islam, from its desert heartbeat, the camel and horse presented the means to an almost unprecedented mobility once the prophet Mohammed had received the first instalment of the Q'uranic text, courtesy of the Angel Gabriel at Mt. Hira in 610, his Hijra to Medina in 622, the conquest of Mecca, the edification of the Kaaba. By 632, the year of his death, North Africa had largely been won over to the cause of Allah. The Shahada, as one of the 'Five Pillars', was a straightforward monotheistic statement of faith ("There is one God, and Muhammad is His Prophet"), and the moral imperatives of the other four: Prayer (Salat), Fasting (Saum), Charitable Giving (Zakat) and Pilgrimage (Haj) were uncomplicated; the straightforward submission and observance to these divine commands guaranteed a passport into paradise. For many this satisfied the natural yearning for communicating with God and satisfying His injunctions. It had a kind of universal appeal, shorn of abstract speculation to which the Holy Christian Mysteries are subject, or the vain superstition which had been common practice in the wider world. Having been embraced by much of the Sahel region of West Africa, on the back of the Trans-Saharan trade: gold from the rainforest south; salt, spices and silk from the north transported, as Bovill poetically relates, by the 'Caravans of the Old Sahara'; the ' Golden Trade of the Moors'. So much of our knowledge of these great Empires derives from the panorama painted by the erudite Islamic Andalusian historians, notably Al-Bakri, eleventh century, whose detailed accounts in 'Kitab-al-Masalik wa-al-Mamalik' as derived from Arab/Berber traders, trans-Sahara, is an invaluable source on ancient Ghana.[25] The great Sudanic Sahelian empires of the middle ages, successively Ghana, Mali, Songhai, had flourished, and Islam had provided a suitable vehicle, structurally based, for the reinforcement of their own kingly power. The fabled cities of Gao, and in particular of Timbuktu, on the Niger Bend, were both principal entrepôts for the exchange of goods, the latter becoming a renowned centre of academia. Here the Emperor Mansa Musa of Mali had established its respected university as a centre for Arabic and Islamic scholarship in sub-Saharan Africa. Hence our detailed knowledge of these medieval states, and the extent of Arabic scholarship. Another Islamic scholar, in Al Bakri's tradition, Abd el-Saidi's 'Tarikh es-Sudan' writing in the seventeenth century, provides us with invaluable chronicles of Songhai's achievements. Despite its impressive cavalry capabilities, Songhai's defeat at the Battle of Tondibi in 1591, at the hands of Moroccan powder-fuelled fire-power, within shouting distance of Gao, is symbolic, but the empire struggled on, much weakened in the respect it had once commanded. Accordingly, by the mid-seventeenth century, the demise of each of these successive empires, ultimately due, in no small part, to the separatist ambitions of client states, had left behind a collection of loosely associated groupings, perhaps with a common allegiance to Islam, but no centralised authority. This, in consequence, had led to a decline in moral values of certain elite groups, whose adherence to Islamic precepts had been reduced to a veneer.

The result was the unleashing of the phenomenon known as the Fulani Jihad (Holy War), spearheaded by Uthman dan Fodio between 1804 and 1808. This was initially a grass roots revolt by Hausa peasant agriculturalists, widely spread throughout the savannah grasslands south of the Sahara, against their own Hausa overlords, a protest in the face of exploitative and corrupt practices inflicted upon them. The peasants were inspired by the seeming purity, as advocated by the Sunni Wahhabist emphasis and interpretation of the Islamic faith. Dan Fodio, primarily a peripatetic Islamic scholar, was a Fulani whose people were themselves naturally wandering pastoralists with their distinctive breed of cattle, and therefore opportunistic communicators. Such was his charisma, that Dan Fodio gained almost messianic status, for the Shi'ite branch of the Muslim sect as the Mahdi, the ever anticipated saviour, the lost Imam. Taking up arms, using the Arabic term 'Jihad' ('struggle') as used in the Q'uran in both its literal physical application as well as its spiritual personal wrestle with one's conscience, the religious zeal of Dan Fodio's disciples helped carry the day. An Islamic Caliphate was now to be established at Sokoto, bringing about a centralised authority across the North, and with it the cement that the accompanies the Faith, with Emirs appointed as lieutenants in important areas such as Kano, and even embracing some Yoruba clans to the south, where Ilorin stood as a kind of religious flashpoint[26]. So, with the advent of British power in the region, the policy of Indirect Rule suited the Northern regions. Leave the newly established Islamic structures in place, including taxation policies, simply bolted on, and guaranteed in return for the acceptance of British supervision and ultimate sovereignty. Leave them to it, end human trafficking, and accept our overlordship. Plato's Republic revisited: British the 'Guardians', Emirs the 'Auxiliaries' and the people, the 'Workers'; a Platonic ideal, simplistically applied as Lugard saw it.[27]

It was the disparity between the culture of the north and that of the southern sector which confronted the British colonial authorities in the twentieth century. The problem was that while 'Indirect Rule' suited the Islamised North, the contrary was true amongst the more diverse cultures of the South, many of whom had embraced Christianity, with its inclination towards an individual path to salvation. Moreover, in its effort to extend Indirect Rule to the south, the colonial authorities had sought to place as client chiefs those who were deemed acceptable and reliable, but who commanded little or no respect from the native populous at large amongst the Igbo in particular. Likewise with the Yoruba, Christian influence and westernised educational systems brought with it a kind of national consciousness, demanding a greater level of self-rule for Nigeria, but with simultaneous tribal overtones and ethnic rivalry. Political parties had emerged, each claiming to advance a progressive future. Under British rule, several attempts had been made to thrash out a constitution for the unwieldy country. Inter-Tribal jealousies frustrated a successful implementation. Not until 1954 was a quasi-acceptable compromise reached: A Federal Nigeria comprising three semi-autonomous regions, plus Lagos as a federal capital territory.[28] It was broadly ethnically based: The vast Northern Region, corresponding to the predominant Hausa/Fulani tribal element; The Western Region based on the Yoruba interest, and the Eastern Region serving the Igbo majority. Lines were drawn in an attempt to encapsulate, neatly, the desired outcome … rather like the victors at the Versailles Conference in 1919 trying to reapportion the former German and Austro-Hungarian Empires equably amongst the successor states, and with the same predictable unsatisfactory outcome. Thus it was at Independence in 1960, as based upon the General Election the year previously. The political parties themselves tended to be tribally rather than nationally representative. The Action Group (A.G.) largely captured the Yoruba following, led by Obafemi Awolowo; Nnamdi Azikiwe had evolved into a leadership role within the National Council of Nigeria and the Cameroons (N.C.N.C.), with a largely Igbo orientation, and the Sardauna of Sokoto, Alhaji Sir Ahmadu Bello, a great grandson of Uthman dan Fodio, the leading light of the Hausa/Fulani Northern People's Congress (N.P.C.). Predictably no party secured an overall majority; a rather unholy coalition was patched up between the N.C.N.C. and N.P.C. The upshot of this was that the Sardauna, preferring to secure his power base in the North, chose to serve as Premier of the Northern Region, leaving the party's deputy, Alhaji Sir Abubakr Tafawa Balewa to take on the role of the national Prime Minister at Independence. In 1961, to complete the picture, as result of a plebiscite in the former 'Trust Territory' of neighbouring British Cameroons, the northern, mainly Muslim sector voted for union with Nigeria's Northern Region, the south opting to unite with former French territory of Cameroon. At Nigeria's independence, as a consolation prize, Azikiwe (Zik) had been accorded the honorific role as Governor-General, and subsequently as titular President in 1963. Divisions within the Action Group over co-operation with the Federal Government between Awolowo and Chief S.L. Akintola was acrimonious to say the least, and led to huge political hot air being banded about among the student body at the University. 'Awo' was seen by most as the 'purist', Akintola as a political opportunist, becoming Premier of the Western Region. As for Anthony Enaharo, a veteran campaigner for the nationalist cause, he was consigned to the relative background in his mid-western following. This was how we found the state of Nigeria when we landed on March 27th 1965.

It was almost with a tinge of envy as we lined up in the corridor of Nigerian bureaucracy, subjected to the heat-induced mechanical efficiency of the khaki attired Functionaries checking our Passports and letters of Accreditation, as we watched the remnants of our 'Deck Companions' ushered through without ceremony, quick as a flash, but heading goodness knows where. Professor Oliver had warned us about this: the virtue of patience and sensitivity would be called for at this point. 'You'll need it!'. Dead Right. Yet we made it through Immigration control, Customs cleared, Passports stamped, into the forecourt where much to our relief Tony and I spotted a white Datsun emblazoned with the University of Ibadan motif: must be for us. We momentarily and shamefully lost thought and sight of David and Ian, who were presumably surveying the carpark for a piece of similar good fortune albeit with Ife in mind. Our Driver, from the Ibadan University Transport Dept., introduced himself as Festus Bamgbelu, in the course of which he navigated our way through the confusing meleé of downtown Lagos, preparatory to the 80 mile drive north towards Ibadan which we reached by early afternoon. Our arrival at the University, our immediate destiny hailing into view, heralded by its clock dominated slender white tower, our formalities at the Admissions Office were fairly peremptory. It appeared the student study bedroom room assigned to us in the designated Hall of Residence was not ready, so temporary accommodation would be arranged at the Senior Staff Club for a couple of nights. This was where the academic staff from diverse departments could mingle socially, and where spare rooms were set aside for visiting dignitaries. The atmosphere around the bar and swimming pool in the evenings was clearly designed to assist Senior Staff to unwind and to let any emotional stresses incurred in the course of the day all hang out. As arranged, by Friday, we were duly escorted to Azikiwe Hall, as befitted our student status, which would serve as our home for the term.

AT THE UNIVERSITY

The epicentre of our West African experience; how privileged we felt, Tony and I, having formally enrolled as alumni of Nigeria's oldest University; the alma mater, after all, of Chinua Achebe, acclaimed Nigerian author of 'Things Fall Apart', a narrative with its contextual focus on the pre-colonial experience of South Eastern Nigeria, roughly Igboland, co-incidental to the first contact with Europeans in the area. Published in 1958, the work has been listed as Time Magazine's 'One of 100 best English Language Novels of all time'. In many ways Achebe was a soul brother of ours, having previously studied at the University of London prior to taking a degree in English at Ibadan's 'UCI' as was known colloquially at the start. Be that as it may, 'UI' as it is now designated, was founded in 1948, in the aftermath of the Second World War, its conception spawned in part as a response to an increased global awareness, alongside the calls for greater indigenous responsibility for the country's infrastructure and governance.

In the same way by which Gibraltar has been frequently referred to as a slice of England, but warmer, in the Mediterranean, so Ibadan University's incarnation had become effectively a piece of the University of London in the tropics. Initially styled the University College of Ibadan (UCI), its tentative beginnings as an affiliated College of London University's Federal Structure, UCI's compound, carved out of the rainforest reflected and replicated writ large the campus idea of Britain's older universities. In fact the virgin territory out of which it arose was to embrace an area of several square miles, its nomenclature reflecting a juxtaposition of colonial and nationalistic sentiment. Housed, as stated, in Nnamde Azikiwe Hall of Residence for Men, our new 'home' had been named in honour of the first Governor-General, and later President, of an independent nation, which had been celebrated in 1960. Tony and I were assigned a shared study bedroom for two, in common with our fellow Nigerian students with whom we quickly became acquainted, on the first floor of a large complex. Despite the tropical variations which dictated the pattern of the day: breakfast served from 6:30, academic business between 8 a.m. till 1 p,m., then lunch followed by 'siesta' to accommodate the extreme heat of the midday sun, until resumption of classes from 4 till 7, in many respects, so familiar was the ambience, routine, and expectations, we could well have been in Commonwealth or Connaught Halls back in London: daily room cleaning and laundry service, central refectory for meals, familiar room accessories; swivel chair each, reading lamp, joint sofa, comfortable beds, bedside tables upon which reposed our mandatory bottles of the Daraprim anti-malarial tablets to supplement the mosquito proof screens shielding the window slats. The communal bathroom was mercifully close by, given the unfamiliar diet to which we were at first unaccustomed. Breakfast was 'ok familiar', with the option of eggs, sausages, baked beans, toast and a cereal option. Midday and evening, though, was initially 'something else'; quality cuisine, judging by the vibrantly fit demeanour of our fellow students, but at first not conducive to the familiar roast and two veg regime upon which we had been brought up, leading Tony to confess that over the course of a couple of days, in consequence, he was "in and out like a weaver's shuttle". Root vegetables, fufu style, was the staple, yam, often served as 'Amala', a concoction of this ground-up tubular delicacy, the equivalent of the Irish potato; accompanied by Opada (usually boiled) Rice and fried plantain serving as the extra vegetable. There was often a cassava option and sweet potato as well. It seemed everything was drenched in palm oil serving as a kind of gravy. Fresh fruit, pineapple predominately was a welcome dessert, along with a generous serving of semovita (semolina, the British equivalent, again a dish derivative of the local soil).

The Writer at Main Entrance to Ibadan University

Azikiwe Hall of Residence, University of Ibadan

Our scheduled meeting on the Monday with the Head of History, Professor J. C. Anene, author of 'Southern Nigeria in Transition, 1885-1906', furnished us with our individualised programmes for the term, its content closely mirroring our SOAS curriculum. A tall, trim impressive figure, distinctly taciturn and succinct, as Prof. Oliver had led us to expect, Prof. Anene's interaction with us was business-like and to the point: a routine ritual, with tutors assigned, essay requirements expected, lectures on offer, social regulations: the usual stuff, without elaboration. We were soon to discover what an impressive bunch of academics he had accumulated in his relatively short tenure of office to date. Still largely staffed by expatriate specialists, there was, nevertheless, the impressive Nigerian lecturer A.E.Afigbo, whose 'The abolition of the Slave Trade in Southern Nigeria, 1885-1950' is a groundbreaking evaluation of the colaboratve relationship between the British colonial and indigenous 'paramount chiefs' in condoning an unofficial internal slavery. Afigbo is a recognised authority on the Igbo contribution to Nigerian nationalism. A.F.C. Ryder lectured on the reign of Peter the Great as well as developing into an authority on modern Africa; as such, the author of 'Benin and the Europeans, 1485-1897', and R.J.Gavin, specialist in post-Medieval European History. Then there was, to my mind, the most academically gifted of them all: J.D. Omer-Cooper. A short, dark haired, lively man, dapper in his customary white cotton shirt and shorts, 'J.D' was our principal tutor for the period. Encyclopaedic in his knowledge, he was at home lecturing on the Rise of Afrikaner Nationalism, as on Plato to Marcilio de Padua, or the Rise of the Forest Kingdoms in West Africa: a Renaissance man in his range of expertise, Omer-Cooper was seldom happier than holding court in his tutorial seminars, habitual cigarette to complement his comfort zone. Midway in the course of delivering a lecture to a packed audience in the Arts Block Auditorium on 'The Breakdown of Marxist Economic Determinism in Russia' he sensed his performance was lacking a level of dynamism. Accessing a packet of Marlborough Lights from his pocket, and cadging a flame from a student in the front row, followed by a momentary pause punctuated only by that initial satisfying drag which accompanied his verbal affirmation, "Ah … that's better!", the lecture did indeed proceed with an enhanced degree of interactive engagement. After his stint at Ibadan, he subsequently served as a Senior Lecturer at Otago University in New Zealand before concluding his career as History Professor at the University of Zambia, presumably assuring the continuing economic viability of successive tobacconists.

Our daily pilgrimage from Hall to the Arts Block sessions, where the History Dept. exercised its functions, technically entailed a circuitous trek around the purpose built macadamised roadway via El Kanemi Road, Jaya Avenue, Niger Road and on to Sokoto Avenue; a bit of a fag, really, en route to a tutorial with J. D .O.-C. A few days in, a fellow Nigerian inmate of our Hall, in similar circumstances, initiated us into an unofficial shortcut: a footpath which had been illicitly hacked out of the bush, thereby cutting the distance by half. My first day attempting this furtive enterprise alone featured an unnerving encounter verging on the traumatic. There, lying in wait for me, as if in prescient anticipation, frustrating my progress, stood the largest lizard I'd ever encountered. It was grotesque: At least nine inches worth of a reptilian incarnation, by my estimation, with blue body and tail, sporting a menacing bright orange head, daring me to advance at my peril, as if in retribution for my so fragrantly testing the boundaries. Frozen to the spot for what seemed an eternity, by chance a fellow student approached from the opposite direction, at which point the errant creature scuttled harmlessly away into the bush: "Common as dirt around here" observed my 'saviour', "Harmless little creature". As I was to discover over the ensuing months: an Aguana apparently, male of the species. Lesson learnt.

An Agama Lizard, such as encountered by the Writer blocking his progress on a narrow path (innocuously as it turned out).

The magnificent K.O.Dike University Library, so named in recognition of the respected Nigerian Historian, Vice Chancellor of the University and former Principal at Fourah Bay, is iconic in its striking yet sensitive profile blending as it does within the context of the campus. It is the standard picture postcard image of the University and that for which it stands. Adequately airconditioned out of respect for the students engaged in their work therein, and for the voluminous collection of books and manuscripts of which it is the custodian, the staff were both knowledgeable and obliging, conscious of its responsibility: calm and an oasis of peace. That is until this one particular day. A student at her desk looked up and horror of horrors, espied an intrusive Black Mamba snake curled up, half asleep, in the roof trusses directly overhead; Panic Button pushed, mass exodus, the ancillary ground staff summoned. Within five minutes a casual maintenance guy rocked up as if from nowhere on his bicycle, wheeling it inside the building, parking it beneath the offending serpent; then, calmly reaching up, courtesy of the enhanced elevation occasioned by a reading desk, he removed the offending reptile, wrapped it around the cycle's handlebars, and pedalled off without further comment. End Of. Equilibrium restored.

The K.O.Dike Library, University of Ibadan

For relaxation Tony and I indulged our fondness for tennis. We patronised the liberally endowed sports facilities on campus, regularly engaging each other just after lunch, to use up the excess calories competitively on court, most days, adjacent as convenience would have it, to the Arts Faculty Block. Even the locals were in awe, not so much of our skilfully executed backhand volleys, nor the Aces served up, but by our regular sessions at that time in the heat of the day, something in which even they, who were used to it, would not indulge at that hour. Nevertheless, climate-wise, how they reiterated the relief felt collectively by the passing of the November to February dry 'Harmattan' season characterised by winds heading southwards from the Sahara, accompanied by the inevitable dust particles irritating skin, eyes, mouth with resultant respiratory ailments associated therewith. We, as it turned out, had arrived just at the start of the 'wet season', March to October: equally hot, but characterised by the regular occurrence of a sudden gust of strong moist wind from the south followed by a violent storm derivative of convection currents: thunder, lightning, torrential downpour, which nevertheless cleared and freshened the air. We paid the price out there playing tennis in the open at this time: Tony more than me. His fair skin was vulnerable and burnt easily, later peeling off in layers when he showered.

Religious inclinations were adequately catered for on site. A purpose built Catholic Chapel which Tony patronised, and a separate Protestant venue, the Chapel of the Resurrection, to cater for my persuasion, had both been tastefully erected, in addition to a Mosque, each of which stood as a testimony to the eclectic clientele as proclaimed in the University's Charter. Endowed with a fine organ the Protestant Chaplaincy was served by an ordained scholar from the U.K., Rev. Stephen Smalley. A Sunday service at 9:30 a.m. was the norm, in English, the lingua franca, with the option of additional worship at 7 p.m. in the languages of Yoruba, Igbo in addition to English. On the evening of Good Friday, April 16th, a pre-recorded performance of Handel's 'Messiah' was offered at the Chapel: The soothing assurance of Job's rendition of faith in the sublime soliloquy 'I know that my Redeemer Liveth' fed into my inscrutable sense of 'one-ness' with fellow students as I made my way in the mystical darkness with the soft cooling breeze as natural companions, along Jaya Avenue back to Azikiwe Hall.

As it happened, a regular member at the 9:30 Sunday service was H.E. the Governor of Nigeria's Western Region as it then was, Sir Odeleye Fadahunsi, accompanied by entourage, and Bentley parked outside, bedecked with national flag. Reflecting the parlous political atmosphere of the Western Region in particular at the time, one visiting preacher's sermon openly criticised the 'Political Establishment' in the presence of His Excellency who was seated ostentatiously in the congregation, challenging the Governor publicly to resign his prestigious office. The collective audible congregational gasp was palpable. H.E. didn't take the 'hint' … not then, anyway! Across the open tract of manicured grass stood the Mosque. Open planned, this was a delightfully designed blend of the modernistic and the traditional; no pictorial representations of the Prophet, of course, but a discrete melange of typical Arabic patterning: a monument to the Islamic Faith embraced by those students from Nigeria's northern areas and beyond, whose worship services likewise would have utilised elements of the Hausa tongue in addition to the obligatory Arabic, and doubtless some English as well.

With one of our fellow residents at Azikiwe Hall we became well acquainted; an expatriate, but far different in terms of background and circumstances. This was Moses Groenewald aged around 25. He hailed from Windhoek in South-West Africa (now Namibia), then subject to the pernicious apartheid regime of South Africa. A tall slender amalgam of Herero and Afrikaner ethnicity, hence officially defined as 'Coloured' in his native homeland, Moses had been subject, therefore, to the degrading segregated second-class citizenship as decreed by the South African authorities of the time. By virtue of his impressive intellect, he had secured a U.N. scholarship to pursue further studies at Ibadan with the academic freedom to pursue his interests such as would be denied him at home. Sadly he hadn't fitted in particularly well with his student peers at Ibadan. Lonely, and emotionally fragile, Moses latched on to us, and we became quite close. It was obvious he was depressed, and our conversations almost invariably and understandably centred around his own misfortunes along the lines of what was to happen to him when he finished at Ibadan? If only we could secure him residence in the U.K. it would be "the dream of a lifetime". He clearly underestimated our capacity to give effect to this aspiration, but we did have more positive times together on occasions: socialising in the Students' Union Bar, retelling of yarns on his visits to our study bedroom in the evenings, and walks around the extensive campus. Ironically, through this personal interaction, we gained for ourselves an incisive insight into the wider areas of the issues confronting 1960s Africa as a whole. We promised to stay in touch after a somewhat emotional farewell in June: a promise we mutually kept, with Moses' correspondence a catalogue of the ongoing frustrations to which he was subjected: insufficient food apparently, and lack of support from the U.N. Thus it was, until a letter I had sent to him from Belize, where I was working by this time, around 18 months on, was returned to me, with a succinct, almost curt, accompanying note from the local U.N. agency in Lagos stating that, 'Mr. Groenewald has passed away'. It was only later that I heard from Tony, who was by now pursuing his PGCE at Makerere University in Uganda, that Moses had sadly, in fact, taken his own life. It was another of those personal stories which, writ large, represented one active testimony in respect of the dilemma faced by so many across the continent, contingent on the fallout of colonialism.

Just down a narrow, nondescript road from us, about a mile and a half distant, David and Ian were ensconced at the even more recently established University of Ife (now the Obafemi Awolowo University). At the time it was temporarily located on the site of the former Ibadan College of Arts and Sciences, pending completion of a soon to be relocated permanent campus in Ife itself, the city of sacred and ancestral significance to the Yoruba speaking people[29] As such, at the time, its pro tem makeshift features and facilities were visibly Spartan, yet for all that, David's and Ian's residential experience was far more intimate and personal than ours at Ibadan. At a more ethnocentric Yoruba based institution with barely a quarter of Ibadan's globally cosmopolitan student body, we reckoned our two friends were perceived as novelties, "sticking out like a sore thumb", as Tony put it. Admittedly, their accommodation consisted of, and comprised, the 'hand me downs' of the former College: wooden stools served as an armchairs, and thin mattresses as bedding comforts; naturally, no longer in keeping with the image of the new place in prospect. Nevertheless, our friends were overtly included and pretty well feted in everything that was going on, plus. In today's parlance it was 'positive discrimination', much of it laid on for their delectation. Imagine, for example, our surprise when we showed up for an unscheduled visit only to encounter our colleagues each sporting a blue academic gown, they having just returned from participating in the summer's graduation ceremony with all the trimmings as specially invited guests. It was a case of Ian's and David's seduction into the full gamut of an integrated communal life, or, as in the luck of the draw, for Tony and me, carving out a niche for ourselves, taking total personal responsibility, navigating a path in the traditional University 'grown up' style: six for one and half a dozen for the other.

Most weekends we took ourselves off into Ibadan, a city whose fortunes and identity were bound up with the enterprise and acumen of the Yoruba. The Bedford Single Decker Omnibus, serving us well at a shilling return, plied the shuttle from the University into Town. It was well patronised by students, the ancillary campus workers and assorted personnel at stops along the way. Queueing at the terminal bus stop was not a recognised strategy to be employed: it was just a scramble to secure any available seat before the vehicle had come to a complete standstill, without due regard for the passengers wishing to alight. The 20 minutes or so into the city centre, served as entertainment as the frazzled conductor vainly sought to collect fares from passengers who were equally single-minded in engineering diversionary tactics in order to frustrate his purpose. On our arrival downtown, in the main shopping street, we recognised we had come face-to-face with the then largest conurbation in Nigeria.

The city of Ibadan, distinctively Yoruba, can trace its ancestral cultural and spiritual heartbeat to the sacred city of Ile-Ife some 50 miles to the east, where according to folklore, the Yoruba origins lie, in the 'Garden of Eden', whereat Oduduwa, the supreme deity, served as creator of the world, leaving his First Lieutenant, Obtale, to fashion the first human beings from the virgin clay.[30] Thus were born the 'Chosen People', Yoruba of course, whose self-assurance in later times spurred them on with missionary zeal to expand their influence amongst disparate clan groupings in the rain forest belt, absorbing them into their self-proclaimed enlightened culture. Symbolised materially, this show of power was exemplified by the universally admired bronze images cast by the 'lost wax' process of the artisans, and the distinctively fashioned terracotta heads. As so often happens, however, unchecked expansion is risky. Leaders of the subject client communities, with ambitions of their own, tend to usurp authority, all the while retaining the mystical substance which they manipulated to ensure the loyalty of their own respective subjects. So while the 'Ife factor' had seeped into the Edo culture far to the East, it was the Kingdom and Empire of Oyo, under its Oba, the Alafin Orumputo which assumed leadership of the Yoruba states by the seventeenth and eighteenth centuries, embracing, at its greatest extent, territory roughly from modern day Dahomey to the environs of Benin; from the River Volta to the Atlantic Coast. In the meantime the intrepid Portuguese and Dutch were chancing their arm along the Bight of Benin, establishing trading stations at Porto Novo and Whydah, in pursuit of trading opportunities with indigenous leaders with whom they could do business. The effect of the firearms deals pulled off with the Europeans was to reinforce the Alafin's control over his own subjects for the purpose of internal stability, yet it clearly posed a menace to his neighbours, and Oyo's military control over much of the region. Worse was to follow. The Alafin's trading links provided the ideal outlet for getting shot of recalcitrant citizens, and prisoners taken in the course of local inter-clan warfare, to feed the incipient demand for slaves on the other side of the Atlantic. To be fair, this activity began as a by-product of Yoruba warfare, and not a cause of this military activity. Yet, the system devoured itself … Increased demand for slaves, more firearms necessary to capture them, civil war in Yorubaland which lasted until a pan-Yoruba Peace Accord was agreed; better to bury the family hatchet, and mount a defence against the common threat posed by the forward Fulani ambitions from the North, but not until as late as 1886. This was long after the Slave Trade itself had officially perished by Act of the British Parliament in 1807, which had given way to more legitimate trading arrangements, but the warfare had continued. This is where Ibadan utself features big time.

Panoramic View of Ibadan City

Founded in the 1820s, Ibadan was established primarily as a Yoruba city of refuge for those displaced by the civil instability, and as a base camp for assorted army factions, all relative to the endemic civil warfare being waged in Yorubaland . Its military ethos, reinforced by Ibadan's seven surrounding hills serving as a natural line of defence, acted as a deterrent to Fulani designs on the region from the north. It was this respite for which many of the war-weary were desperate to beat a hasty retreat. Furthermore, situated as it was on the cusp of the rain forest to the south, and the savannah flatlands to the north, its geographical location was to stimulate the development of Ibadan as a trading centre, with its natural defensive topography, and with potential access to the Atlantic coast and the native kingships further to the north. The settler refugees still clung to their historic Yoruba ancestral cultural and religious heritage, harking back to the legendary Oduduwa of Ife.

With the increased activity of the British on the West Coast throughout the nineteenth century, based on their established toehold in Lagos, came further opportunities for profitable trade. Following the Berlin Conference, Sir George Goldie's Royal Niger Co. was determined to assert exclusive British authority in Yorubaland. In 1893, with the connivance of the Olubadan of Ibadan (the spiritual and titular heir to the Yoruba Onis of Ife, the Alafins of Oyo, and the Obas of Abeokuta), such was the prestige of the city by this time, the British Governor of Lagos Colony proclaimed a 'Protectorate' over several of the Yoruba states. With the legal unification of the northern states and the southern entities of this disparate sphere of British influence by Lugard as a defined 'Nigeria', in 1914, it was clear that the Yoruba ethnic grouping would play a key role in determining the future development of the Protectorate throughout the course of the 20th Century. The problem of its form of constitutional governance was to exercise the skills and diplomacy of its respective Governors and colonial officials and the various indigenous hereditary, or their spurious equivalents, colonial sponsored office holders; the agencies and tools inherent in the principle of Indirect Rule. That, and the need to hold in tension the increasingly more vociferous demands of an educated elite for democratic concessions leading to people power and self-government. Ibadan, as the economic centre of gravity of the educated, progressive, pragmatic business-like instincts of the Yoruba people, it was to be a significant player in the various experiments in drafting the various constitutional arrangements over the period of 40 or so years. As stated above, the ultimate compromise was for a Federal State at Independence, comprising three federal regions, to correspond with the three major ethnic groupings: Hausa/Fulani as the Northern Region; Igbo to form the basis of the Eastern Region, with of course the Yoruba based Western Region with its capital located naturally in Ibadan: all very neat on paper, but really a Balkanised attempt to square the ethnic circle: the incongruency of drawing convenient neat lines through (and enclosing) amorphous, divergent and historically antagonistic disparate ethnicities. Trouble stored up for the future; already by 1963 the Western Region executive, and the city of Ibadan which housed it, had been perforce to concede the cession of its eastern extremities, the Bini and Delta areas, to be transformed into a fourth entity, the so named Mid-Western Region with its capital at Benin City.

Our forays into Ibadan led to the appreciation of a people, proud of their inheritance, yet judiciously adapting to the wider national interest: the city exhibited a sensitivity to both. Downtown, the business centre boasted the recently constructed Cocoa House, built on the back of the lucrative cacao export trade, soaring to the heavens as if in gratitude. Thus emerged the first 'skyscraper' in Nigeria, where deals were struck, fortunes to be made, and modern technology applied to facilitate slick trading arrangements in the traditional time honoured tropical resources of the soil. Public transport was served mainly by suburban bus travel such as we accessed to venture into town and back. The taxi drivers were almost aggressive in their touting for trade; no fixed fares, one had to strike a hard bargain in the event of being persuaded to surrender to the initial seduction; as we did when wishing to observe the city from one of its seven peripheral hills. The one rule the municipal authorities insisted upon was that taxis must be furnished with four doors. Historically the smallest, and therefore the most affordable such vehicle, was the old black Morris Minor. Plenty of them, but there was evidence that the Japanese Datsun was beginning to take over, being more stylish and comfortable as befitted the status of the up-and-coming local entrepreneur and status conscious taximan.

From the vantage point of the Bower Memorial Tower, erected in 1897 to honour one Captain Bower, British Resident to the Ibadan District of Yorubaland, proclaiming on a now heavily tarnished plaque the "Loyalty of the Yorubas to the Imperial Crown", the panoramic horizon of the city was apparent: a vista of row upon row of closely-knit traditional mud huts, thatched roofing having been replaced with corrugated metal rusting with age: hence the nickname applied to this, the most expansive conurbation in Nigeria, as the 'City of Brown Roofs'. On the face of it, things seem to have changed but little since the days of Captain Bower: sheep, chicken, dogs, wandering nonchalantly in the side streets and alleyways; goats munching on the grass at the side of the road, often in mutual combat for possession of the limited resource, so typically in contrast to the swish main street in the aforementioned business centre in town. Here the Dept. Chain Store, the ubiquitous 'Kingsway', the Debenhams of West Africa, offered an air conditioned respite from the heat outside; all the normal wares one would expect on display; expensive, and occasionally weakening in our resolve to avoid temptation, we purchased the odd souvenir or two against our better judgement, but at least avoiding the hassle of having to haggle for a sharp price for similar items outside in the heat. Furthermore, the smartly dressed, mostly female, counter assistants in European or Yoruba style outfits, were so charmingly 'civilised' in their dealings with potential customers; who could resist? Conveniently for us, a few doors down, a large projecting Union Flag proclaimed the presence of the British Deputy High Commission; reassuring to us in a way, if we came unstuck. We never needed, fortunately, to avail ourselves of the consular services on offer, save to pick up our mail from home as a 'Poste Restante' after we had decamped from our University base at the end of term. Further down the street on the opposite side, was the well appointed 'Leventis' Supermarket; again a chain outfit, operated managerially by a Lebanese concern, who some years previously had sensed a suitable outlet for its inherent business acumen; local and imported essential foodstuffs were to be had for a fair price, and we certainly took advantage to supplement our diet. The urge to patronise Nigerian enterprise was never allowed to escape one's notice. 'Ah! ... Star!' ... Proclaimed the giant billboard every 50 yards, hitting us between the eyes urging us to ' Buy Nigerian', profiling two young good-looking dudes happily toasting each other, pint glasses clinking: the product of Nigerian Breweries founded as far back as 1947 competing with the equally appealing, but imported, Heineken advert, slightly smaller, a few feet away. For the temperance minded, targeting the other gender this time, was the indigenous milk fruit-drink poster, extolling the virtues of 'Fan' as manufactured by the Nigerian enterprise, Fandango, screaming its delights opposite, covering the entire shop window of a convenience supermarket; superimposed by the seductive pose of a young lady, unlike the window, barely covered. As we jostled our way on the sidewalk with the shoppers, mostly women, at this hour of the day, many carrying their infant offspring, as custom dictated throughout West Africa, tied to their backs, plus inanimate possessions perched precariously on a panier on their heads; others more pretentiously sophisticated, parading their fecundity sporting the latest fashion statement in wheeled perambulation, we habitually patronised a little side street coffee shop on our trips into town, introduced to me by a fellow American student at the University. According to him, the cafe was a 'bit of a dive', but we found it a congenial watering hole, run by a couple of young married locals, budding entrepreneurs, who seemingly took an interest in our own background, and who filled us in on the latest city goss.: a decent beverage to be had, without paying Kingsway's more impersonal inflated restaurant prices.

With arrangements to be considered for the end of term, and our weeks of travelling in prospect, a visit to the local Wesley College seemed a useful point of contact. My membership of the Methodist Church could prove potentially handy in respect of providing us with useful references as we were to journey around for what for us was unchartered territory. Methodist Mission Stations had been established widely throughout Africa in the nineteenth century. The social emphasis accompanying the fundamental assertion of John Wesley that 'All need to be saved; All can be saved; All can be saved to the uttermost'[31] had struck a positive chord with a fundamentally spiritual people reeling from the aftermath of internal conflict consequent upon the vicious demands of the Slave Trade. The Gospel was, if you like, Gilead's healing balm (Jeremiah VIII, 22) applied to a festering sore. With it had come new opportunities founded on compassion, service and peace. Co-operation with the European traders with their outlets to the wider world for the natural products of the region had been attractive, with ensuing profits to be made, shorn of the misery inflicted by the iniquitous trade in human flesh. That had had educational implications: the need for literacy, as a vehicle for a more sophisticated intercourse with the industrialised world, overlaying the fundamental task of instruction in the essentials of the Christian dynamic. Wesley College at Elekuro on the outskirts of Ibadan was one such product, founded initially in 1905 as a training centre for teachers, and subsequently morphing into a co-educational government sponsored secondary school: the school whose alumni included, beloved of the Yoruba, "man of the people", Obafemi Awolowo: articulator early on for the Independence imperative, Leader of the Action Group in both Regional and Federal Parliaments, and later still, Finance Minister in the Federal Government. At all events, It seemed opportune for us to make our presence known. Accordingly, around Whitsuntide, the anniversary associated with Wesley's own 'Warmed Heart' Aldersgate conversion experience (May 24th 1748), we hired a Morris Minor Taxi to Elekuro on spec, and without appointment, introduced ourselves, explaining our circumstances. A somewhat bemused receptionist phoned the Principal's Secretary who provided us with phone contacts and addresses in Kaduna and Jos. Ad hoc formalities concluded, with no further ado, we were politely ushered out: busy time, obviously. It nevertheless focussed our minds on preparation for our pos- academic sojourn in the tropics.

It had, in fact. been a Methodist connexion that prompted our first venture outside Ibadan since our arrival. Mrs. Hannah Moore, a member of Central Methodist Church in Eastbourne and wife of Mr. Eric Moore, Headmaster of Willingdon Secondary School back home, had been involved in teacher training in the U.K. One of her previous students, a Nigerian, Mrs. Solomon-Omage, now worked as a mentor/counsellor to students herself at Ibadan University, and we were armed with a personal letter of introduction. Consequently I became good friends with Mrs. Omage and subsequently with her husband, who happened to be big on Scouting, a shared interest. Of Edo ethnicity, round face, firmly focussed eyes, short in stature, immaculately turned out in a cotton print dress when we rocked up one evening, unannounced and unexpected, letter in hand, at her apartment on campus she shared with a seven year old daughter, she seemed genuinely pleased to meet us. She later kindly invited both of us to spend a weekend with them at their family home in Benin City, capital of the aforementioned newly created Mid-Western Region. Accordingly, we set off on June 6th. The resultant mile upon mile, around 150 of them distance covered, west to east, visibility compromised by torrential rain, was, in itself, hair raising; Mrs. Omage at the wheel of her Volvo, taking the central (only) lane on the highway as if a latter day Stirling Moss; Tony at the rear, and me in the passenger seat up front, with hearts in mouth audibly palpitating. "Precious lives", was the good lady's attempt at reassurance, in good faith, I'm sure; not that that, in itself, would have made a great deal of material difference should we have encountered a likeminded Lewis Hamilton addressing us from the opposite direction. We survived; both ways; miraculously without a scratch, as had my Grandfather in the course of his tour of the duty on the Somme in 1916, but with his nerves shattered; his permanently; ours, mercifully, ephemeral. The Omages' comfortably appointed two storey detached house in Benin City betrayed a family of well-to-do proportions: a live-in 'Steward', Friday by name, and a servant girl, Usoma, whose role was to attend the female requirements of the Mum and Daughter of the household.

Mr. Solomon-Omage, a tall, solidly built man of business, smartly dressed in suit and tie, was clearly someone of importance in the city, on good terms with Oba Ekenzua, Edo tribal elder at Benin City since 1933, with whom he had arranged an audience with us the following day. The Oba could claim descent and heredity by virtue of the sacred medieval/clan social hierarchical structure characteristic of common West African practice.[32] Up until the nineteenth century the Edo had proudly maintained a distinctive measure of relative autonomy. Following, again, endemic warfare amongst neighbouring clans, the Kingdom, surprise surprise, had become caught up in the repercussionary web and fallout of the Berlin Conference.[33] The British, whose influence had in any event been established by Missionary contacts, had been 'upset' by the then Oba's reluctance to engage in meaningful trade negotiations, as expressed by some violent resistance to such overtures. The upshot was a punitive British expedition in 1897, from the coast, to redress the 'wrongs' perpetrated by this 'upstart'.[34] The disgraceful episode climaxed in a pillaging of the city by troops on the rampage, reminiscent of Charles V's soldiery's rampagious Sack of Rome in 1527. The ancient defensive earth walls, the world's most extensive structure of similar nature, having been constructed over period of time during the medieval period, were breached and destroyed; just a few remnants, now mercifully restored, to remind us of the extent and pride of this noteworthy political entity whose influence at one time extended as far as modern Ghana. Culturally Benin had perfected the ancient art, probably inherited from the erstwhile Yoruba connexion, of the lost wax process of brass moulding[35]. The exquisitely sculpted head and shoulder images had been sacreligiously looted by the incursive troops, and many are still to be seen in museums around the world. Pleas to restore some of them (resonance of the Elgin Marbles' ongoing saga) from the British Museum to their contextual origins have been heeded, for which Ekenzua must take due credit. The centre of Benin City, surrounded by closely knit huts, straddling narrow streets, is designed to focus on the Oba's Compound itself. Hardly 'palatial', either in dimension or imposition, this is but a material replacement for the performance of the bare essential functional duties of an Oba with mystical divine pretensions, the 14th Century original of which was destroyed by the vandals, in 1897. The destruction of Solomon's Temple by Titus in A.D, 70 would have borne witness to a similar cultural outrage. It was here, at any rate, in this clay based edifice, that our audience would take place; all credit to his Eminence that he would grant a couple of young British a measure of hospitality in the light of all that had transpired close on eighty years previously. Mr. Omage had prepared us with the due protocol to be observed in response to the gracious invitation. We were received at the entrance by the male 'page', clothed solely in khaki shorts, presumably the status of eunuch being no longer a qualification for the job. We were ushered into the presence, where Ekenzua himself reclined on what appeared to be a padded ceremonial stool. In this relatively small reception room, walls adorned with pictures of revered ancestors, the Oba came across as informal, dressed in white traditional cotton robes, incongruously chain smoking whilst he fielded our questions with the educated panache of a man who was plainly having to balance the demands of the new world with the sacred traditions of the old. We were accorded a peep into the altar room, at the focal point of which the ceremonial sacrifices were presumably still offered. Disturbingly the remains of a chicken carcass and a plethora of feathers reposed in the hearth. Rumours of human sacrifice way back in times of yore were not hard to imagine.[36]

On then to the outside world, into a city which today is famed for its dazzling array of bright colours. A rich dress culture is self-evident among the rising middle class, the women adorned with accessories in the form of arm bangles, anklets, beads, necklaces and facial markings. The city had certainly capitalised and prospered subsequent to its capitulation to the British; the abundance of rubber, derivative of the rain forest had been exploited to feed the western car industry, and crucially the oil boom was just beginning to take off. We paid a visit to the small museum of exquisite Benin terracotta statues housed in Idah House, close by. This was so named after a victorious historic encounter in the fifteenth century waged by Oba Esigie against a challenge posed by a chief of neighbouring Idah who resented Esigie's attempts to compromise the sacred native religion by embracing at least elements of the Portuguese import of Christianity as had been entertained by Oba Ewuare, around 1490. All of this was influenced by Benin's embrace of the cowrie shell economic culture by which the Portuguese ironically capitalised as a medium of exchange which had been introduced into West Africa by the Arabic traders back in the eighth century, and which was by now common currency throughout the region. The shells had become prized both as a symbol of mystical properties and as an attractive item of jewelry. Derivative of the source of these 'gems' based upon Poruguese colonial enterprise in the Indian Ocean, and subsequently by that of the British and Dutch, one could argue that it was a case of an exercise in classic capitalism.[36a] Hard by the Market Square stands the statue of Emotan, a historic matriarch verging on Mariolatry in Edo folklore; she who played the part of Caesar's wife by warning Ewuare of mortal danger, yet in Emotan's case the warning heeded, saving both throne and life. Such is the richly and jealously guarded history so dear to the Edo people. The veneer of tradition is preserved. As with all of Nigeria's historic rulers, to many the Oba represents the soul of the tribal clans. The format is retained, but their constitutional power has given way to a western adaptation of parliamentary democracy. They are consulted, and they perform historical ritual, providing a colourful defining reference point for the sustenance of the clans' identity; an analogy to the Commonwealth role of the House of Windsor and its Realms, would not be far off the mark.[37]

Ebony Wood Carvings, courtesy of Benin City artisans

Our host then guided us around the highlights of modern Benin City, passing the modern Parliament Building housing the then legislature of the Mid-Western Region; a stark contrast to Ekenzua's homely compound. The traditional artistry of the Edo wood carvers was in evidence as we watched them at work in their craft shops. Beautiful ebony figures were being turned out in the style of the bronze statues of yesteryear. I bought a delicately carved ebony head, about 4 inches tall, and an ebony elephant of similar dimension, each at an advertised price … no haggling … and a further one or two appropriate souvenirs for the folk back home. I still have the carvings which have taken up residence as centre pieces on my desk. Next day, being Sunday, we attended 7 a.m. Mass with the Omages - they were Catholic. Well actually we were there by 7:45, too late for full participation, but it was apparently a common occurrence, and in the great scheme of things it was 'alright', because we had, in fact, 'heard Mass'. Then lunch, prepared by the servant girl and served by Friday (not the day of the week, but the Steward), after which Mrs. Omage refuelled the Volvo as we edged our way through the remnant of the venerable ancient walls of the city, steeling ourselves, for the return to Ibadan in one piece, thankfully, by 8 p.m.

It had been an interesting first-hand expose of the ethnology of the region. The origins of the present day tribal groupings are clouded in oral tradition. Olaudah Equiano even claimed to have been of Igbo ethnicity[37a]; he who was abducted from the 'Benin Kingdom' mid eighteenth century, despite the evidence of a more Edo based tradition prevalent in the region today. Scholars are themselves divided as to the genesis of the Edo identity. Even in very modern times, the Ekan, another tribal grouping of the Mid-West, have distinctive Edo features, from which the 1950s proto-nationalist campaigner, Anthony Enaharo, descends, allying himself at one point with the Yoruba Obafemi Awolowo's Action Group in pursuit of meaningful national Independence. Ryder[38] is content with the thesis of the early Edo association with its Yoruba foundation, based upon linguistic analysis. This, coupled with common customary social observances, is my preferred interpretation. Be that as it may, the tribal clan groupings have evolved into self-proclaimed distinct entities, with huge implications for modern Nigerian politics, not least it being the catalyst for the fractious partial dismemberment of the Western Region and the creation of the 'Mid-West' of but very recent memory.

Back at the University, we had a couple of weeks to wind up our academic affairs, submit our final essays and prepare for our departure at the end of the month. The regular students in their third year of residence were in the throes of their 'finals', the last under the auspices of the University of London, prior to Ibadan's initiation as a degree awarding body in its own right. By chance, a visiting external moderator had flown out from London, for a couple of weeks, to lend credence to the application of the examination assessment criteria. This happened to be G.S. Graham, Rhodes Professor of Imperial History at King's College, London, whose course in the subject formed an intrinsic part of my own undergraduate programme. I took a gamble, one evening, and looked him up in his room at the Senior Staff Club. He seemed genuinely pleased to renew our acquaintance, spending a congenial couple of hours sharing a bottle of Nigerian whisky, which he just happened to have opened, and feeling somewhat the worse for it next morning; he too, as he confessed, when we next met at KCL at the beginning of the Michaelmas Term in September.

On the 26th of June having previously thanked the academic staff and the ancillary operatives who had served us so well, we bade farewell to our fellow students in Azikiwe Hall as term ended, Tony and I keeping open the option of ad hoc informal residence thereat on our return from our travelling excursion across Nigeria. Likewise we wished Ian and David all the best, as their own plans, far more ambitious than ours, was to encompass intrepid river travel on into neighbouring Francophone Nations to the North East. "Regular little Mungo Parks", was my injudiciously insensitive remark to Tony on learning of their itinerary. "Hope they don't end up like him", was Tony's equally infelicitous response. They didn't.

The plan and objective of our own venture was to explore, however briefly, the sheer diversity of the country such as had been thrown together as a direct consequence of that fateful Conference in Berlin. That forms the next part of the story.

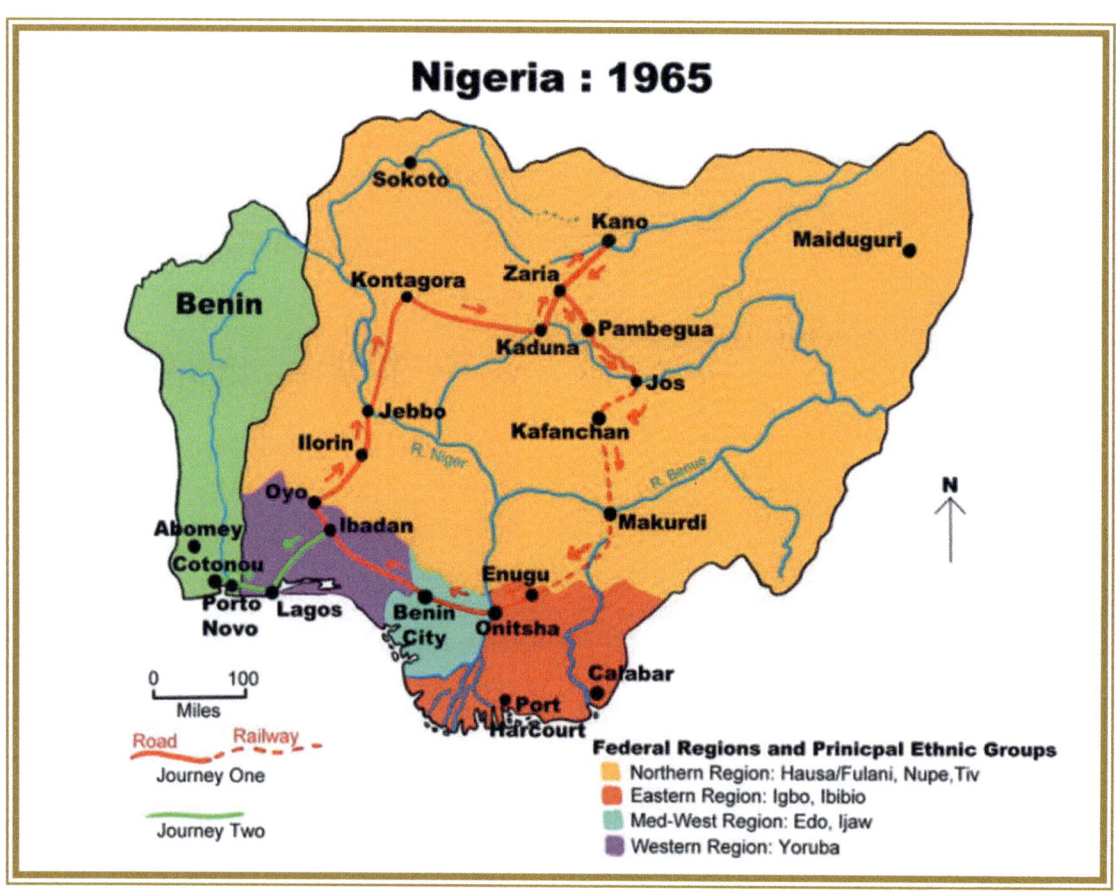

Nigeria, 1965 Writer's Itinerary (map drawn by Anouk Berryman)

June 26th: Time to go for it. Tony and I having left the relative domesticity of the University, and Azikiwe Hall in particular, we showed up at the long distance lorry park in Ibadan, Thomas Cook Travellers' Cheques safely secured to our person. Here we seemed to be spoiled for choice. Trucks of all shapes, sizes, colours and ages: the trading life-blood vital to the sprawling nation, many in the process of disgorging their sacks of maize for distribution to the metropolis; others loading their produce, piled high and jammed to the gunnels. Many of the conveyances boldly and unashamedly proclaimed 'No God but God', presumably not just an Islamic Mission Statement, but serving as a talisman for Divine protection on a long journey. It was accepted practice that passengers could be accepted to accompany the commercial enterprise, and hopeful drivers competing for our custom. It wasn't long before we were persuaded into accepting an offer from a young(ish) Hausa operative, dressed in native attire, standing beside the cab of a red Volvo truck about to head North. It was obvious from our experience by now that here was the opportunity for him to cash in on the extra remuneration derivative of two young hopefuls, who by virtue of their colour, shall we say, doubtless had the readies to guarantee some additional pin money. Our objective for the day was to reach Ilorin whereat Tony had had the foresight to arrange an overnight stay at the presbytery of the Catholic Bishop. We were duly offered the passenger seats at the front, with the open load of sacked bailed-up merchandise perched precariously at the rear.

Navigating the by now familiar thoroughfares of downtown Ibadan, we hit the open road, familiar structure by now: a one tarmac laner, with parallel laterite 'hard shoulders' either side to allow for passing traffic from either direction. With our vehicular experience in the company of Mrs. Omage fresh in our minds, our thoughts were already contemplating the eventuality of an incident on a highway such as this. Such a morbid prophecy translated into fulfilment when we encountered, 15 miles out, the immediate aftermath of a confrontation involving a time-weathered wooden slatted sided truck (a 'Mammy-Wagon', in local parlance) laden with produce heading south, and a black Volkswagen Beetle, now frustrated in its northbound destiny. Road blocked, a couple of Fulani herdsmen navigating their long-horned cattle round the wreckage adding to the complexity. No serious injuries sustained fortunately, but a three and a half hour delay was incurred before the police and breakdown crew facilitated progress. By midday we had arrived at Oshogbo, a relatively small country Yoruba town, but with past profile of significance in the twilight days of the Oyo Empire. It was here, in 1840, that the northern Fulani military advance was halted by an Ibadan sponsored militia, frustrating its avowed thrust towards the coast.[39] Here our driver decamped momentarily, with prayer mat in tow, kneeling by the side of his truck in observance of the Muslim Prayer Ritual at midday. As we motored on northbound, the dense rainforest gradually gave way to savannah type topography which was typical of the intermediate Sahel region south of the Sahara.

Arriving at Ilorin at around 4:30, 85 miles from Ibadan, we headed for the Bishop's residence where we were greeted courteously by Mgr. Omahoney, an Irishman, who was expecting us, albeit somewhat earlier, refreshed by a generous helping of tea and cake; our first taste of food since breakfast at the University. Pleasantries thus exchanged, we were shown around the mission station, agreeably located as it was on the perimeter of the city, set in a few acres of greenery. We parked our rucksacks in our allotted room, and waltzed off into town, heading for the Government Rest House for supper. To our misfortune we were destined to share a table with two fellow expatriate types, financiers apparently, who exhibited less than effusive appreciation for the indigenous colleagues with whom they were forced to rub shoulders in the course of their work. In sotto voce, we were regaled by tales of their recent encounters of the 'uncivilised' morality and manners of the 'locals'. This encounter took the edge of what was otherwise a pleasantly served up meal consisting of a steak and kidney pie followed by a generous helping of pears and cream, washed down by coffee and mints to finish: all very 'civilised', actually. This establishment's concession to the cuisine of European tastes was a pleasant antidote to the company of our boorish compatriots. Thereafter we strolled back to the Mission House, about a mile, taking in the relatively peaceful night-time urban ambience of a Yoruba city, characterised in Ilorin by its thatched ochre mud houses, served by several small mosques located at intervals. We let ourselves in to the Bishop's residence, careful not to disturb the already sleeping hierarchy, tip-toeing into bed quite late.

Ilorin is something of an enigma in modern Nigeria's evolution. Yoruba by nature, its betrayal of vassalage to the traditional Oyo heritage by its local chieftain in 1829, aided by Muslim Fulani mercenary cavalry forces, led to the installation of Abdul Salam as Emir of Ilorin, subject to the Islamic Sokoto Caliphate.[40] His expansive ambitions beyond were only halted by dogged resistance marshalled by the Ibadan force at Oshogbo in 1840 already alluded to. The Central Mosque, golden domed, with its symmetrically spaced quadruple minarets at each corner, dominates the city centre. It's a city of commerce, a central market and outlet for crops of the local soil: groundnuts, rice, sorghum, millet, cassava, yams. Resisting British pressure until the Royal Niger Company's subjugation of nearby Bida in 1897, the Ilorin Emirate was attached to the northern provinces of Lugard's Nigeria, for 'Indirect Rule' purposes. Thus, at Independence, in 1960, despite voluble protestation from some quarters, it was slotted in as an integral part the Northern Federal Region: the only area, containing the only sizeable Muslim conforming element of the Yoruba speaking people, for historical reasons, not to be associated politically with the Western Region of Awolowo and Akintola.

Next day, after an early rise, we duly indicated our gratitude to our hosts, and made tracks for the central Lorry Park in town. By chance, en route, a driver of apparent Lebanese extraction pulled up beside us in a blue Peugeot saloon, asked us where were heading and if we would care for a lift. It so happened he was heading 50 miles north as far as Jebba on business, part way towards Kaduna. We were grateful for this slice of good fortune. Solicitously replacing his own luggage into the boot, so as to accommodate us for our convenience, we set off in good spirits. The highway layout was familiar: single track, laterite hard shoulder; fortunately at this juncture no mishaps to impede progress. It was noticeable as we sped on, that the vegetation was now giving way quite overtly from tropical rainforest to more open savannah parkland, and the evidence of human activity therein based on the increasing number of straw huts at the side of the road. We made good time, reaching the Jebba Bridge spanning our first sighting of the River Niger by 11 o'clock, 50 miles on. Here there was a fortuitous delay as we waited for the all-clear to cross its width, all 1,700 feet of it. The multi-purpose bridge happened to be playing host, at that hour, to a freight-cum-passenger train powered by time honoured steam locomotion, reminiscent of the 'School's Class'; itself being hindered by a crossing of yet another herd of some 50 or so Fulani beef cattle, being guided to their appointment with the slaughterhouse down south in no particular hurry, it seemed, to savour their Aristotelian eudemonia.

What a magnificent vista, as we looked down on the translucent blue waterway below us, on that gorgeous sunny morning as the mighty river rolled inexorably on towards its famous delta before spewing its essence into the Bight of Benin! On either side, its banks entertained small fishing communities, existing in a kind of Wordswothian pastoral idyll, but with no evidence of the solitary reaper, despite the pentecostal rhythm accompanying the agrarian activity far below.

Fishing on the Niger at the Jebba Bridge

Jebba Town, encompassing both North and South banks of the river, is believed to have been founded by one Okelere Leiloke and followers fleeing the aftermath of the fall of Old Oyo in 1735. Hence it has Yoruba in its veins, while its geographical position established the town and hinterland firmly within the Muslim northern ambit.[41] It was close-by that the Scotsman Mungo Park, in his ultimately futile quest to trace the course of the Niger and its links to the Congo, capsized and drowned in 1806.[42] A memorial to his intrepid yet ill-fated expedition has been erected in the town. Its strategic location at a critical juncture on the Niger being within some equidistance from Britain's sphere of interest in the north and south, provided a suitable military base for the Royal Niger Company's operations in the latter half of the nineteenth century. Jebba also served as temporary capital of the newly created Northern Nigeria Protectorate by Lugard from 1900 to 1902, following its submission to the British in 1897. The bridge across the river was completed in 1909, thus providing a vital rail link between Lagos and Kano, via Ibadan; the bridge, the structural aesthetics of which we had ample time to appreciate.

A Mammy Wagon awaiting repairs, Tony in the rear, the Writer up-front

The bridge, when finally divested of its erstwhile clientele, cleared our passage; once across, onward and upward acknowledging the giant anthills on the side of the road, towards Kontagora, which was as far our kind benefactor was going. We took advantage of the break to patronise a small native restaurant at which we were served up a traditional meal of amala, fried plantain, cassava, semovita; by this time we were adapting quite well to the indigenous cuisine, not least because we were pretty much ready for anything. The afternoon was nevertheless wearing on, and Kaduna some distance yet. The lorry park was the obvious place to take our chances. In the meleé we hailed a truck packed high, as per normal with sacks of root flour in its open cargo hold, and sporting a boldly indicative motif proclaiming the Islamic Shaddah that 'There is one God, and Mohammed is His Prophet', about to head off. Yes, the Hausa driver was passing Kaduna; yes, at 12/- a head he would convey us to Kaduna. Rain threatened, and Tony unselfishly insisted that he would be prepared to brave the open elements, aft, allowing me the relative luxury of front passenger seat travel, squeezed alongside the driver's companion. Such being the unkempt nature of highway maintenance at this point, the journey of 182 miles turned out to be an eight hour trek. When we did eventually hit the outskirts of Kaduna, which is where we were unceremoniously discharged, 4 miles out at the city airport car park, around 10:45 p.m., no, the driver couldn't take us any further. What to do? Close by was what appeared to be an army barracks; maybe a spare room for the night, as we ventured to ascertain this sanguine possibility at the gatehouse. "Halt! ... Who goes there?" a disembodied barked command slowly materialised out of the pitch black background apparently morphing into what transpired as a tall uniformed officer as he emerged with due formality from the sanctuary of his sentry box. In similar clipped tone he suggested that for our own good we move on pretty quick if we knew what was good for us ... or words to that effect; sensitive area and all that. We took the hint and deflated, we hit the highway once more. Fortune nevertheless smiled upon us as a passing taxi miraculously spotted our desperate attempt at hitching a ride into town: price no object. Please take us to the Methodist Missionary's House, that being the only vague contact we had, and no advance warning that we were either expected or anticipated; not even that the minister had ever even heard of us. As we pulled into his drive, at around 11:30, the house was in darkness, although in response to the sound of tyre on gravel, a set of lights illuminated the interior, and whom we assumed to be Rev. and Mrs. Johnson appeared at the front window in night attire. "We're from Wesley College", was all Tony could proffer by way of explanation for this bizarre encounter. That must have pushed the right button, as a kind of password, for it had the desired effect. To our amazement, the Rev., almost without hesitation, opened the front door. "You'd better come in then", he suggested. Within minutes a cup of tea was provided, a few words of introduction exchanged after which we were ushered into the spare bedroom where two beds enveloped by mosquito nets were as only prescience would dictate, ready for occupancy, as if we had been expected all along: no fuss; The Lord had certainly been gracious unto us, we felt, as we drifted into slumber.

Up and dressed the next morning at 6:30, we made our first meaningful interaction with Rev. and Mrs. Johnson around the breakfast table, over American style pancakes, maple syrup and coffee. The Rev. had business in town early on and accordingly dropped us off in the city centre, leaving us free to ingest the atmosphere and spirit of this, the administrative federal capital of the Northern Region.

The city itself had been conceived by Lugard for geopolitical reasons, and had been open for business as the Northern Protectorate's capital since 1917, it being on the hub of transportation links. A key factor here was its strategic position on the Lagos to Kano rail link with its interaction with trade on the Kaduna River, itself a tributary of the Niger; suitably accessible and equidistant to and from other parts of the vast expanse of Northern Nigeria. Thus evolved in effect a synthetic metropolis; what might have been termed, in post-war Britain, a 'new town'.[43] Kaduna expanded rapidly, attracting mainly a Hausa/Fulani workforce to service its rapidly growing commercial concerns such as are wont to accompany its political status. Its planned street orientation would have borne favourable comparison with Hausmann's Paris. Initially Kaduna served as a distribution centre for the natural products of the surrounding savannah grassland: Sorghum, Millet, Groundnuts (of course), tobacco even. Cotton, thus cultivated, led to the development of a flourishing textile industry, capitalising on the natural indigo dyeing process which has produced the distinctive colours of the flowing northern native attire. Likewise the city has provided a convenient marketing centre for livestock: cattle, sheep, guinea fowl and chicken, all suitable for raising on the surrounding savannah topography. The Islamic influence is nevertheless overt. Mosques abound, sensitively blending the traditional architecture with modern air conditioning systems discreetly in place. As a quasi-external creation of recent conception there is no traditional Kaduna native authority of any note within the city itself; all this is more evident in the more rural entities outside the urban administration to this day.

This became apparent as we wandered the planned environment which was open to us. Lugard Hall, built to a twentieth century design, home at this time to the Region's legislature; Colonial Court Houses, still displaying the Royal Coat of Arms of the House of Windsor. We took coffee at the Leventis Restaurant, and paying, again, an unscheduled visit, this time to the British Council where we were received with polite disdain. It was then back to the Johnson residence for lunch, where their steward had prepared for us all a melange of African and European fare: Joloff Rice, Beef, all topped with Palm Oil, followed by Fruit Salad and Cream. Over the meal, Rev. Johnson gave vent to his frustration to the lack of a unified approach to Christian Mission amongst the variety of denominations which had once vied with each other for attracting converts to their particular brand. He was praying for the go-ahead for a signature to a memorandum of understanding with the Anglicans at the upcoming Conference of the Nigerian Methodist Church, paving the way for unity and a public declaration of common purpose. It was not to be, and as far as I know, no organic union has yet taken place. This hasn't surprised me; a Yoruba Methodist of some prominence, Mr. Adesanya, whom I later met in Lagos, was to declaim that he was "Methodist to the Core": not untypical of your average punter raised in the Wesleyan tradition. Nigerian Methodism's one concession to change has been its more recent adoption of an episcopal formula for administration: Bishop This, Bishop That. It's difficult to see how this ties in with genuine application of apostolic succession as claimed by Catholics and Anglicans. Perhaps, nevertheless the titles and form appeal to tribal communities with their penchant for hereditary spiritual and incarnational embodiments as in the semi divine persona of Obas, Onis, and Alafins.

After lunch, we were 'entertained' to the slaughter of a couple of the domestic chickens by the Johnsons' steward; presumably to grace the lunch table the following day. Meanwhile it had been been arranged for us to dine with the British Council resident, Mr. Lambert and his wife, that evening, and to kip down for the night at the home of David Pullen, a 21 year old graduate who was spending the year under the auspices of the British Volunteer Programme's sponsored Voluntary Service Overseas (V.S.O.). He was teaching English and Humanities under the scheme, which provided accommodation, living expenses along with a token salary: a comparatively new venture at the time, similar in principle to John F. Kennedy's Peace Corps initiative. It certainly appealed to my own sensitivities and worthy of serious consideration for my own future path when graduation duly dawned eighteen months hence. Such it was to be. David Pullen appeared to survive in relative comfort, with a steward employed to prepare his meals. Post-prandial, we soon fell asleep on the air-beds (no netting) on which the steward had expended excess breath on inflating. As if in in vicarious appreciation we spent a restful peaceful night.

The following morning we rose promptly at 6:30, deflated our airbeds (no netting to worry about this time). David's steward prepared for us a hearty breakfast, for which we left him a few shillings gratuity as we departed. The British Council, by chance, had a car going as far as Zaria that day, and they had arranged to give us a welcome lift to this historic city, a welcome stop-off point en route to Kano, a good 150 miles distant, our most northerly destination. The rain was tipping down in buckets as we were leaving, but cleared up shortly after we hit the open road, which was in the process of being treated to an upgrade by an Italian outfit; much needed infrastructure linking north to south if Nigeria's vast economic potential was to be realised to the full. We pitched up at Zaria's Ahmadu Bello University, impressive even by Ibadan's standards, at something before 9, in good time for a pre-arranged meeting with Mrs. Eileen McArdle, a Senior Admin. Officer at this recent foundation, appropriately named after the then Sardauna of Sokoto, now Premier of the Northern Region. She selflessly gave up her morning to take us on a guided tour of what, for me, was the most aesthetically and culturally attractive of the towns and cities we visited, its ancient walls, adobe compounds, and clay houses are adorned, Islamic fashion, with vivid, vibrant ornamentation.[44]

Zaria, Walled City

As with most cultures, the Yoruba for example, as we have seen, this Hausa city has an oral tradition which has its semi-divine origins bearing witness to a treasured folklore preserved down the centuries. The story runs that during the tenth Century a refugee from Baghdad, Bayajidda, pitched up at a Sahelian village, Daura, where its inhabitants were being terrified by an evil snake which limited their access to water. Bayajidda, with nothing much to lose, took on the snake barehanded and slew it; problem solved; a la David and Goliath, George and the Dragon. The young man was rewarded with the hand of the 'Queen of Daura' by whom he had six sons. The family then, by tradition, respectively founded the 'Seven Hausa Cities' of which Zaria and Kano remain the most prominent. Such is the stuff of legend, which serves as a kind of catalyst for collective cohesion; as such its Islamic credentials are palpable. The Hausa states thus evolved thereafter into scattered but autonomous entities in the Sahel, yet retaining, like the Yoruba and Edo further south, a common thread of cultural and religious consciousness and practice: hierarchically structured, with a quasi Emir presiding. More likely, these Hausa communities were originally derivative of the medieval Mali/Songhai Empires of the Upper Niger, agriculturalists primarily, having absorbed the Muslim creed from the historic trans-Saharan trade in gold, salt, and regrettably the slaving enterprise ultimately serving the Corsair purposes in the Mediterranean. Uthman dan Fodio's Fulani Jihad, 1804-08, to which reference has already been made, resulted in Fulani dynastic Emirs replacing the Hausa variant; clients of the Sokoto Caliphate.[45] Despite this, the Fulani consequent immigrants were absorbed into the Hausa culture to mutual advantage: the products of the soil, the ubiquitous sorghum, millet and maize; the lifeblood of the Hausa agriculturalist economy, benefitted from the advent of the Fulani cattle which served as a valuable fertilising agent. Zaria. The city and surrounding area had been absorbed relatively peacefully into Lugard's Northern Nigeria, having sought 'Protection' from endemic slave raiding from its Kontagora neighbour in 1901. The Sokoto

Caliphate as such, was, by now, for practical purposes, ineffectual, and was formally wound up by 1903 as the region's supreme authority. A classic version of Indirect Rule ensued, with Zaria's economy beginning to reap some of the benefits of a secure regime. The growth in cotton production and, the associated traditional indigo dyeing techniques, did much to enhance Zaria's socio/economic prospects in the twentieth century.

Already we were feeling the pervasive Islamic influence, as we managed to hitch a ride to Kano with an Italian Executive of the Italian Road Firm constructing the renewed highway. Anxious as he was to sing the praises of his company's achievements as he pointed out en route some of the technical intricacies of construction, much of our vocal interaction was one-sided. We were nevertheless grateful for the lift. Held up for an hour at the bridge over the Kano River, the customary Fulani herdsmen cajoling their charges with limited success and with little concession to the demands of a society with deadlines to meet and deals to be struck, we pondered to what extent their traditional way of life could be sustained in the light of the commercial advances we had witnessed in Zaria, as Nigeria advanced technologically into the modern world. At least the interlude offered us the chance to observe the rhinos nonchalantly luxuriating in the cooling waters below us, blissfully oblivious to the plight of the human species caught up in a time warp yards above them. We arrived on the outskirts of Kano around 4 p.m., impressed immediately by the spaciously wide boulevards which lent access into the city. The view of the central Mosque hove into sight, to which all roads seemed to gravitate, its double fronted minarets casting their watchful eye over the faithful and infidel alike. This was so typical of the all-embracing Islamic culture which we had come to expect from this archetypical Muslim city over which the Fulani Emirate had expended much of its largesse during its period of pre-eminence. Uthman dan Fodio's heart would have danced to learn of the extent to which his Islamic idealism had been translated into practical expression, embraced and respected even under, or indeed because of, the umbrella of the British pragmatism of Indirect Rule.

Like Zaria, Kano claims descent from one of the sons of Bayajidda, and as such claims its place as one of the seven Islamic Hausa cities. Subsequently it is claimed that another of its Sultans married into the family of Askia the Great in the mid 1460s. Around this time the present Emir's Palace was built, and the extensive city walls around the old city constructed, some 12 miles in extent and between 30 and 50 feet height. Leatherwork, cloth and metalware were traded in exchange for for salt and spices from north of the Sahara. Slaves were also a profitable commodity way into the nineteenth century by means of the trans-Saharan caravan routes to the north African coast, long after the trans-Atlantic version had ceased. The city's Muslim character was reinforced by its submission to the Fulani Jihad in 1805, when the last Hausa Sultan was replaced by the Fulani Emirate subject to the Caliph of Sokoto. Its profitable Sahelian trade continued and remained undisturbed until the Emir submitted to British pressure in 1903 with but token resistance when, as with Zaria, the Sokoto Caliphate was abolished. The city's traditional economic base nevertheless continued with minimum disruption during British rule, and commercial enterprise in cosmetics, pharmaceuticals and cement took off in the twentieth century. Ado Bayero had been installed as Fulani Emir in 1963. Again, as in Zaria and across the North, the Fulani have become linguistically integrated into Hausa culture and the embrace of Islam has helped seal this marriage of convenience.[46]

The British Council in Kaduna had furnished us with a V.S.O. contact in Kano, Tom Wells, another English teacher, who picked us up on arrival. His offer to take us on the grand tour was gracefully accepted, passing the Emir's Palace and on to the gloriously appointed Central Mosque standing in a vast open forecourt, its white structure and minarets proclaiming the blessing of Allah upon the city's endeavours. Without touching base with Kano's Mosque and savouring the obligatory view from the dome would be akin to Tony visiting Rome without paying a courtesy call on the Vatican. Mind you, there was a price to pay: all of 12/- to be exact: not the set price, in fact, but inclusive of the usual 'dash' expected by many a local operative in return for a 'favour' rendered; great vista anyway, as we surveyed a sprawling yet seemingly ordered community, its populous largely domiciled in square, flat roofed, sturdy mud built homes. Together we dined early evening in the restaurant pertaining to the inscrutably named 'Hotel de France'; not exactly 'haut cuisine', but adequate for our needs. Back at Tom's for the night, he expanded enthusiastically on the value of responding to the call to volunteering overseas. He seemed to enjoy a comfortable lifestyle, perhaps not commensurate with those amongst whom he had been 'called' to serve. Albeit, he treated us with courtesy, and we bedded down in the spare room, replete with protective mosquito netting, turning in at around 11:30.

The following morning, Sunday, we were up and ready by 8 o'clock. Full English Breakfast was duly served up to the three of us by Tom's Hausa steward, exhibiting a faultless command of English, doubtless honed to near perfection by virtue of his acquaintance with Tom. Tom suggested that the two of us hire bicycles for the day to enhance our appreciation of the vast extent of the city. At 3/6 each, we felt this was good value, a means of transport ideally suited to the flat terrain, by means of which we covered a good deal of ground. A Fulani Guide, Abu, offered to accompany us for the day to ensure we got best value in return for our investment. For 5/- it was well worth absorbing his encyclopaedic knowledge. We took in 'Sabon Gari', for example, a quasi-ghetto for 'immigrant' non Muslim workers from the south, Igbos mostly; a chilling portent symptomatic of the intensifying civil unrest which would erupt with tragic consequences a few months later, and culminating in the Biafran War some ten years further on. We took lunch at a bistro located just inside the 'ghetto', after which we patronised the widely acclaimed street market offering a diversity of wares from dyed fabrics, beads, native calabashes, chickens, guinea fowl, to the produce of the soil: no fixed price for anything, the value of each item being assessed by what the vendor thought he could extract from the would-be client by weighing up his/her likely disposable assets.

Amongst the clientele at the market was a group of men, veiled in blue headdresses, examining the indigo dyed fabrics on offer. Not found in vast numbers in Nigeria itself these folk belonged to the Tuareg tribal grouping, whose tradition of nomadic pastoralism across the Sahara and northern Sudanic regions had come under increasing threat. In any event, their numerical strength of around 2 million is distributed mainly amongst the francophone territories of Chad, Burkino Fasso, Niger, Guinea and Senegal. Of Berber extraction, linguistically, they had embraced Islam, and during the height of the trans-Saharan trading era, they had played an important role in the overland commerce, their camel trains being highly successful in negotiating safe passage. Herders as well, organised into clan groups of anything between 30 and 100, their natural way of life being that of leading their herds to the grazing areas, akin in some respects to the lifestyle of Amerindians of the Great Plains. Traditionally they have been tent dwellers, naturally so in view of their nomadic culture. This has made it difficult to assimilate them into the national identities following 'Berlin', and their failure to grasp the significance of national frontiers.[47] Even today, they are 'tolerated' as such by the independent nations, provided national security is not at risk. Unusually for an Islamic people, the hierarchy is matrilineal, hence the men are veiled and the women are not. This may well be in deference to oral tradition which credits the origins of its people to a fourth century Queen, Tin Hinan. Although they had a tendency to resist French colonial authority, they have never featured prominently in politics or demands for independence during colonial times This participation in the wider political front may increase as larger numbers of Tuareg are taking to a more sedentary life style as agriculturalists as commercial prospects change; even perhaps, turning up as farm labourers or workers in bottling plants in the cities. However, their history is significant as to their role in bringing Islam to the Sahel, and their presence is distinctive in terms of their language and elaborate dress code, the men customarily armed with double-edged swords and leather shields, more so today as a concession to tradition in the fashion of the Scotsman's ceremonial Kilt, Sporran and dagger.

Early evening Catholic Mass attended with Tony was followed by a stroll back to Tom's place where his trusty steward had prepared supper for the three of us alongside another V.S.O., Philip, who had been operative over the border in the francophone Niger Republic and who was en route to the airport for repatriation to the U.K.

at the end of his tour of duty next day. To our surprise, it transpired that, quite by chance the previous week, he had run into our colleagues David and Ian, travelling deep into the Niger Republic; in good nick apparently, not having met Mungo Park's fate: Good to have news of them.

Monday we planned the next stage, which was to head back south by way of Jos on the Bauchi Plateau, thus to take in the Eastern Region, thereby covering the bulk of the country as a round trip. We duly replenished our water bottles, courtesy indirectly of Douglas Lawson, to whom reference has already been made: one-time expatriate water supply facilitator in Kano for 30 years and father of Angela, aforementioned.

Our schedule would mean doubling back on ourselves, part way as far as Zaria, and branching south-easterly from there. Tom generously resisted our offer of recompense for his hospitality. Maybe instead a personal 'dash' for his steward would be an acceptable way of expressing our appreciation for his solicitous regard for our comfort: a suggestion with which we duly complied to express our gratitude. Tom dropped us off at the junction for the Zaria highway where we were perforce to rely on the procedure of 'rule of thumb'; hitching a lift, basically, as ready cash was drying up, and the drivers of the 'Mammy Wagons' didn't take Promissory Notes in the form of Cooks' Travellers' Cheques. After an hour and a half, spent in the company, by the roadside, of two female Peace Corps Volunteers on a similar quest, we bundled, all four of us, into a Land Rover driven by a well-heeled Hausa businessman. A little drama was encountered on the way. At an ambitious 55 m.p.h. through a country village, a fated chicken in the process of crossing our path on the proverbial road, fell victim to our driver's disregard for such niceties as speed restrictions. In a flash, a host of villagers appeared as from nowhere, in consternation in their grief at the loss; not so much at the untimely passing of a dearly loved pet, but at the pecuniary deprivation of the proceeds such a (live) specimen would fetch at the local market. Perhaps we should stop and apologise, was Tony's sensitive empathetic advice. "No chance", responded our driver, who clearly read the situation better than we did: right foot on accelerator rammed to the floor, "Not if you don't want to be lynched!" Looking behind us at the undisguised collective angst of the bereft community, we convinced ourselves of the veracity of our driver's assessment.

On arrival at the now familiar profile of Zaria (second time in a week), as we passed through the hallowed gates of the ancient city around midday, we bade farewell to our Peace Corps companions (did we let an opportunity slip here?). We headed straight to Barclays Bank D.C.O., where we were to pocket some readies in exchange for a traveller's cheque, and from thence to the junction of the Jos highway; positioning ourselves strategically wherewith to chance our arm (with thumb attachment) in the prospect of hitching our second ride of the day. Disabused of our sanguine projections, five hours of frustrated optimism saw our fruitless attempts at progress by the side of the road beginning to wear a little thin. We resisted the temptation to join the mandatory Islamic ritual of daily prayer with which local Hausa/ Fulani were engaged roadside; instead furtive silent personal petitions were proffered to the Almighty, begging forgiveness for past confessed infractions of the Ten Commandments, in exchange for a positive response to our dilemma out there in the heat of the day; that and my own intermittent voluble solo rendition of 'We've got to get out of this place', The Animals' hit single of 1965, much to Tony's undisguised chagrin. At this point, momentarily, our companionship was feeling the strain, either because his musical tastes were incommensurate with my own, or he lacked appreciation of my distinctive vocal style, or perhaps, like mine, his frustration at our predicament was beginning to surface; maybe a confluence of all three. By 6 p.m. we had conceded defeat. The Lord manifestly had other plans of His own for us. Forlornly we trudged back into town, where we threw ourselves on the mercy of the Catholic Mission where at least a welcome cup of tea was rattled up for us, but no offer of accommodation (no vacancies, perhaps). Then inspiration: Tony recalled how Professor Oliver had, in passing, suggested catching up with a fellow academic in the field of African History, and presently a Founding Senior Lecturer at Ahmadu Bello University, where we had called in a few days earlier.

Sheer good fortune put us through to Tony Kirk-Greene at our first attempt from the antiquated phone booth in town. He kindly sensed our predicament, offered to pick us up there and then, offering us hospitality for the night. He had an appointment scheduled at 7:30, so he lent us a couple of bicycles to access the Refectory at the Samaru campus meanwhile, where for a modest 9/6 we dined on roast pork, with all the trimmings; dessert of fruit salad comprising the local papaya, pineapple and a suggestion of ackee. Back at the University, we caught up with our gracious host: Tony Kirk-Greene, a true legend of a man; an alumnus of Eastbourne College, he had spent time as a colonial administrator, a District Commissioner, I suspect. He was fluent in Hausa and now an authority on the History of West Africa and a University academic. It's said that he churned out volumes on the subject, faster than it took for punters to read them. No wonder he and Roland Oliver were soul mates. We tipped into bed at his place around midnight, having caught up on our return, accompanied by a post-prandial drink, with recent research projects on which Tony K-G was currently working. This remarkable man, with his storehouse of knowledge and first hand experience embracing a formative period of British Colonial History, as it merged into a Commonwealth of Independent Nations, lived on in subsequent retirement, till his passing in 2019 at the venerable age of 91.

We paid our respects to our host at around 9 next morning, promising to extend his personal salutations to Roland Oliver on our return to SOAS. We needed to analyse our aborted attempt to gain access to Jos the previous day. A more promising road junction was suggested to us, this time on the corner adjacent to the University's Institute of Administration, where we had previously encountered Mrs. McArdle. Fine; except that our taxi man expected 15/- for a two mile journey to reach it. We offered him 6/-. Significantly he accepted our tender without a murmur! An hour passed ominously, as we watched in hopes for a lift, until a Mammy Wagon, 'Mohammed is His Prophet' style, piled high with sacks of maize and cassava, condescended to stop for us. Tony and I perched perilously on top, clinging on for dear life for 50 miles as far as Pambegua: nothing much more at the time than a bush village, which was as far as the vehicle was going. Jumping down, we were immediately mobbed by a host of local children to whom the arrival in their community of "oyebos" was an obvious novelty. Pleasantries eventually exchanged, an hour and a half ensued by the roadside before the driver of a Land Rover acknowledged our intentions. Yes, Peter Woods, such was the name of this American, was heading for Jos for a short break. It turned out that he was the director of a Diamond Company (Diamonds in Nigeria? … ah, based in Sierra Leone … that explains it). The Land Rover four wheeled drive proved a necessity on this road, characteristically heavily reliant on the parallel laterite hard shoulders on either side. Peter handled the vehicle with the panache of Jeremy Clarkson, as if he knew the co-ordinates of every pothole lying in wait for us, like the back of his pockmarked hand. No nail biting trauma as per Mrs. Omage; thanks, Peter.

We had learned of Jos (J-Town to the British. Jaarce to Americans; Tin-City to both) from one or two of our expatriate fellow passengers on board the 'Apapa' on our way out. Situated almost bang centre of Nigeria, it was their optimum choice to have a bit of a long weekend break, if one's tour of duty coincided with the steamy hot summer months: bit of a 'Mecca', or more appropriately for the British, a 'Brighton Beach', 'Blackpool Tower' or 'Southend' Pier; an escape, where at the same time one could catch up with friends posted to the four corners. At an elevation of 4000 feet, on the Bauchi Plateau, its tropical savannah temperature range afforded a welcome respite. The city's origins, as always, were clouded in the vagaries of oral tradition, but there is certainly archaeological evidence of the Stone Age 'Nok' Culture of around 900 B.C. to 200 A.D, famed for the terracotta images of ancient gods of that period, as were on display at the Museum of Jos Inheritance.[48] Jos, in fact, had never fallen to the advances of the Fulani Jihad, and Islam had never taken root anyway, being further south.(Zangerbadt, L.G., 'History Of Jos and Political Development Of Nigeria'; Dudley, B.J.,'Politics in Northern Nigeria'). Conversely its growth can be ascribed to the influx of non-Muslim refugees, fleeing from Islamic purism as was being imposed elsewhere by the Sokoto Caliphate in the north during the early nineteenth century. Christianity was far more pervasive in Jos. As a result, the very cosmopolitan nature of the evolving city precluded the evolution of a traditional 'Oba'/'Emir' style structural administration with divine credentials even though Fulani herdsmen had begun to pasture their cattle on the plateau owing to the absence of the tsetse fly. Thus, while part of the Northern Protectorate for governmental purposes, the classic Indirect Rule policy was inappropriate for Jos, and a somewhat ad hoc arrangement persisted for the duration of British rule. This cultural diversity was exacerbated by the discovery of Tin on the Plateau in 1904: on the face of it, a sure basis for future prosperity, bringing with it a new influx of mainly southerners, Igbo and Yoruba largely, to cash in on the mining related jobs and infrastructural opportunities on offer. To transport the raw material, the railway was built to link the city with Port Harcourt, itself the product of the export requirements derivative of growing commercial enterprise. Sadly, Independence witnessed a burgeoning inter-ethnic rivalry and hostility; what once had been known as a haven of concord morphed into a den of hatred and violence, sullying its reputation as a tourist hot spot, although it seemed expats were largely spared direct evidence of this, at least during our time there.

It didn't take us long to find a place to rest our heads for the night; a novel quasi-hostel, really: a small compact compound of small round thatched huts, native style. For 6/- for the night we played at a basic existence, going 'native' ourselves, rather in the manner of Marie Antoinette acting out her fantasies at Petit Trianon. In the evening we hired a couple of bicycles to sus out the prospects of travelling to our next port of call, across the Benue, and on to Enugu, the hub and capital of 'Igboland' and of the Eastern Federal Region. We enquired at the Catholic Mission House as to whether there might be the chance of hitching a lift on a diocesan vehicle which just might be heading in that direction next day. We drew a blank there, and so on to the Methodist Communal Centre on Ibrahim Desuti Street, where we sought out the Superintendent of the Jos/Bukuru Circuit, Rev. Ale, whose name had been given to us at Wesley College back in Ibadan. Seemingly anxious to be of assistance, the good Reverend drove us over to the Plateau Pax Hotel, the proprietor of which happened to be a member of his Church: no joy there either. Comfort Food was definitely called for. At the 'Bight of Benin' we were served up with some basic 'chop' (the expatriate term for restaurant fare), before returning to the fantasy world of the mud hut for the night. An early reconnaissance of a possible lift to Enugu, enquiries being made while we took breakfast back at the 'Bight of Benin' offered no realistic prospects. With no enthusiasm for another roadside vigil, we turned up at the railway station, where we booked a passage on the Night Sleeper leaving later that day.

Our steam powered locomotive (was it a former 'Schools' Class? ... not sure ... I didn't have my schoolboy train-spotters' guide to hand) was fired up on our arrival and we were shown to our compartment, a four berther with side corridor leading to washing and toilet facilities. We were warned that at night we should keep the compartment bolted as we passed south toward the Benue. It had been known that this was an area where Tiv criminal activists posed a 'threat'. We never did ascertain the nature of the threat. What was apparent, however, was that the Tiv ethnic community was an endemic victim of Fulani prejudice based upon their lack of structured social hierarchy and sedentary agrarian culture: 'primitive', in their estimation.[49] This could well have accounted for the dire picture painted. Rev Ale waved us God-speed, as we chugged out of Jos revealing a range of jagged hilltops on either side. It was to be a slow process on this single track permanent way for the 300+ mile trip. we agreed on which of the four bunks we would appropriate. Choice of four, two up, two down, Tony one side, me atop on the other; no need for blanket, none to be had anyway. The journey in prospect was to be slow, stopping at stations at regular intervals and halting to allow passage of other trains at designated passing loops. At each stop we were tempted to step out onto the platform to stretch our legs, and purchase victuals: snacks and water on offer from a mass of eager vendors each competing for our custom, along with the assorted sundry items from kola nuts to condoms. No set price, of course, so it was a case of exercising our increasingly refined bargaining techniques. At Kafanchan Junction, where the Jos to Maiduguri branch joined the Main Line serving Port Harcourt and Kano, via Enugu, we encountered a group of destitute children mournfully and pitifully casting their eyes in our direction as we jostled with the masses in pursuit of our own sustenance. One little feller, as I recall, was solitary. He was suffering from the obvious, but not uncommon affliction of elephantiasis: one of his legs was swollen to a bizarre degree making walking a slow painstaking business. I beckoned him over, and offered him a shilling or two, for which he murmured a token of gratitude. I wondered afterwards whether he in fact was to be the beneficiary of my own token gesture, or whether he was a 'plant' for unscrupulous profiteers. The prevalence of beggars throughout our stay in West Africa was a source of conscience. How could one refuse a few pennies to those with little or nothing in the light of my own opulence by comparison? Yet, were we simply feeding the prostitution of the vulnerable, whose circumstance was being exploited by the corrupt practices which were such a prevalent feature of the society? Was this an excuse on my part to hang on selfishly to what, in the eyes of the deprived, was far in excess of my 'needs'? Rev. Colin Morris, recounting his experience in Zambia at the time in his book, 'Include me Out',[50] Morris articulates the dilemma for western society, and his forthright denunciation of western priorities has certainly remained with me as a constant reminder of our Lord's injunction to 'do unto others … '[51].

We were joined, at this same Kafanchan, in our compartment, by a male American Peace Corps Volunteer, likewise heading for Jos. He then took possession of the bunk below that of Tony, opposite. Sleep was at a premium, the assorted array of 'wagons lits' had not been originally designed for the purpose; rather converted from, it seemed, pre-war stock from the Southern Railway. At around 10:30 the customary rumble of wheels over track assumed for a matter of minutes a different characteristic: hollow features suggested air space below. This must be the crossing of the River Benue at Makurdi. It was indeed, as confirmed by our Peace Corps acquaintance peering out of the window from his vantage point on the lower bunk. In any event, the rising heat inside the apartment was indicative of the fact that I had erred in my choice of the top bunk bed. I decamped to the spare lower version before Tony had the same idea. Little difference it made, for lower back muscle spasms had taken hold, not to mention the constant sound of newly arrived passengers in the corridor, as they boarded and alighted at each scheduled (and non-scheduled for that matter) stop.

Accordingly, to say that I woke up next morning misses the point; it felt as though all three of us had been up most of the night, snatching a few winks to punctuate our hours of disturbed bunkering down. First light was struggling to welcome us through the semi opaque blinds, but at least we were consoled by the fact that there had been no sign of the doom-laden Tiv activity, benign or otherwise we hadn't been anxious to confront, such as we had been led to anticipate. As we steamed into Enugu Railway Station at 7:30 a.m., after what seemed to be an eternity, we grabbed our stuff. We weren't keen to take further advantage of the somewhat, by this time, dubious ablution facilities on board the train. Instead our Peace Corps companion suggested we accompany him to the Peace Corps Hostel for our brief stopover in the city. As we made due egress from the station we took a last look at our means of conveyance of the past 12 hours. Sadly, the Jos-Enugu rail connexion has subsequently fallen on hard times, with recent pictures of former rolling stock row upon row, rotting in the sidings. Maybe our own carriage is among the victims. Such a pity, in many ways, that this line, as with others on the Nigerian network has been allowed to deteriorate; its History having played a pivotal part in commercial development. At the Hostel we agreed to surrender 13/- for an overnight stay, after which Tony and I agreed to spend the morning to 'do our own thing', Friends we had become, but having been virtually joined at the hip for a prolonged period we wished it to remain that way, if you know what I mean. Off then to explore Enugu.

The city itself had assumed the role as capital of the Eastern Region by the advent of Independence in 1960. Like Jos, it could not claim to be a hereditary entity of a distinctive ethnic grouping, in contrast to Ibadan's historic Yoruba links in the West, or the Islamic Fulani/Hausa Emirate of Kano in the North. Yet, Eastern/South-Eastern Nigeria has been as distinctively Igbo in its overall identity as have the major ethnically defined groupings of the other regions. It's simply the case that native Igbo administrative governance had been based not upon a quasi-divine incarnation as in Yorubaland, nor upon the Muslim Sharia Ideal in 'Hausa/Fulaniland', but a more ad hoc oligarchic rurally oriented agrarian focus: the satisfaction and distribution of subsistence necessities: cassava, and the ever important yam, whose cultivation approximated itself as close to divine status as the oligarchic regimes would permit. The annual Yam Festival,[52] still observed, is testimony to this throughout Igboland, and in various guises, throughout the Igbo diaspora. It's true, some kind of kingship element did evolve in parts of Igboland, in pre-colonial times, but divine assumptions were never attributed, and such 'Obis' as were eventually recognised, operated in a pragmatic consultative role, rather than by virtue of esoteric mystique. Nevertheless, common oral traditions amongst the Igbo people, served as a spiritual touchstone; interestingly bearing resonance to the Yoruba versions described earlier.

This common thread of this ancestral heritage is manifest in the Igbo 'account' of a divine transcendent creator, Chukuwu, who has communicated to his people by means of lesser deities, through natural phenomena like thunder, and through the performance of arcane ritual, divination and 'consultation' with oracular sources. Protection from misfortune and for that matter vengeance for the infliction of wrongs by others can be sought by means of the wisdom accorded to the 'priestly' class.[53] Small wonder, then, how Christianity found some fertile soil. The Igbo have certainly proved to have been especially amenable to the Christian Gospel, and Catholicism has found a populous amenable to its acceptance. Think how, for example, the Christian tradition was bolted on to pagan Saturnalia, with 'Christmas' timed to coincide with the celebration associated with the passage of the winter solstice. Yet the old stories don't go away. Igboland was again ideally situated for the Slave Trade, and Igbos themselves were both slavers and enslaved in the process. The 'spiritual' traditions have thrived in the Caribbean diaspora, where I subsequently taught for over a decade. 'Junkanoo' at the New Year is a Bahamian costumed celebration said to have its origins in the oblations to the Igbo earth goddess; more sinister, the resort to the 'Obeah[54] who can 'put mouth' on one's enemy for a price, can have its origins explained with reference, perhaps, to a more innocent motivation amongst pre-Christian Igbo. A student of mine in The Bahamas fell ill. All the tests revealed no physical defects to explain her slow deterioration to the point of her sad demise. It was later revealed that she had been the victim of an obeah 'curse' from which she believed there was no escape; effectively she gave in mentally to the inevitability of the 'efficacy' of the 'force'.

The city of Enugu, therefore, grew up as a British inspired commercial centre to which surrounding agriculturalists and others were drawn after the discovery of coal deposits on the surrounding plateau in 1909. With it came the railway linking the city to Port Harcourt, and the importance of the new urban complex escalated as it served as a market place for Igbo agrarian products along with manufacturing enterprise such as bottling factories and metalworks. The prevalence of neo-Georgian buildings in the centre bear witness to the entrepreneurial spirit which gave birth to the modern town. Like Jos, the town had not lent itself easily to classic 'Indirect Rule', it having no recognised traditional indigenous hierarchy through which to channel authority. As part of the Lugard's Southern Province, the city and state were administered by appointed Councils of significant locals and subject to oversight by District Commissioners. Granted 'Municipal Status' in 1956, Enugu was selected as the capital of the Federal Eastern Region just prior to Independence.[55] That's how we found it in 1965, by default irrevocably tied up with the identity and fortunes of the majority and ambitious Igbo. This was to have tragic repercussions in the immediate future and in ensuing decades.[56]

As I wandered through the town, the prevalence of Catholic influence pervaded the ambience. Churches, Shrines and Crucifixes very much in evidence. The discovery of the inevitable Kingsway provided me with an excellent opportunity to catch my cool and indulge in a finely brewed coffee. Settling at a table to savour the serenity and luxury of singular escapism, browsing through the local newspapers on offer, Tony rocked up at the table opposite beside me, with, I suspect, similar intentions. "Well, fancy meeting you here", was his cheery salutation. The introspective spell was broken. An unspoken sense of security was engendered by the return of the familiar which had the effect of reigniting our joint sense of purpose. It provided an opportunity for us to purchase some long overdue postcards to send to our sponsors in London. To Humphrey Fisher, our saintly SOAS Tutor (he was later to be ordained as an Anglican Priest), in order, at the very least, to prove we were taking full advantage of our latter day sojourn after term ended; to update him on said progress, and to assure him that our allowance was not being swallowed up loafing around in some club for expatriana in Ibadan. Off, then, to the superbly appointed Eastern Region Central Library to write them, and to check out the important contribution to locally sourced literature such as we had been made aware at Ibadan. Achebe's 'Things Fall Apart', we have noted already, was set in Igboland, after all![57] His prescient award winning novel details the hopes empowered by the spiritual strengths inherent in the traditional clan structure, the stories with which he would have been familiar growing up in his home town of Ogidi in South Eastern 'Igboland', but which was doomed to perdition by the complexities implicit in adapting to rapid changes and challenges implicit in absorbing alien cultural influences as western colonial advances impinged. In it, Achebe lays bare the wider propensity of humanity's natural desire for positive self-improvement and so-called advancement, but which is so vulnerable in the face of its inherent fragility implicit in the lure of abuse of the blessings with which it has been endowed.

Thus edified, it was back to Kingsway for a brunch in the afternoon, a sausage roll and ice cream (ingested separately) which kept the wolf from the door. Our return to the Peace Corps Rest House was by vehicle shared, courtesy of a volunteer whom we had met in the restaurant. On our way, amidst the neo-Georgian facades to which reference has already been made, we noted the very fine structure of a recently purpose-built hospital. As I was later to discover, Angela, a future colleague and future wife of my latter-day Headmaster Roger Perrin, the daughter of Douglas Lawson, the aforementioned 'water man' of Kano fame, working in Enugu at the time, was the first 'white' baby to be born there, apparently to great excitement at her safe delivery. Our attempt at self-catering at the hostel would have barely passed muster as a contender for a Michelin Star, but as is so often the case in such establishments, one makes the acquaintance in the communal kitchen with fellow travellers on life's journey. One such encounter thereat was Herbert, on the newly conceived VSO Cadet Scheme, whereby the 'gap year' on finishing in the VIth Form at a British Grammar School was taken up on a voluntary capacity in a developing country. Herbert was making ready, at the end of his tour of duty, to commence his undergraduate studies in Social Anthropology at the University of Sheffield. What a superb orientation he had now already experienced by a very practical initiation into the formal discipline!

At 6 a.m. rise next day, a decent bath, self-catered breakfast and a booked taxi, we were headed for Onitsha/Asaba 90 miles distant in a Peugeot by 9. By its very geographical circumstance Onitsha on the East, Asaba to the West banks of the Niger, the conglomeration had become a veritable hub for commerce, industry and education. Onitsha tradition suggests a foundation sometime in the sixteenth, seventeenth centuries by Benin émigrés, establishing a monarchical regime with a hereditary Obi with overtones akin to the Benin model. Thus emerged a semi urban area which was growing up to support a potential natural trading emporium of some stature. This was given a shot in the arm when a Briton, William Baillie, struck an agreement in 1857 with the then Obi by which a trading post could be formally established in the town, given its strategic location on the river.[58] A major Catholic Mission was to be planted firmly in place around this time, which provided us with a staging post in Onitsha. Accordingly we made tracks to the Cathedral Basilica of the Most Holy Trinity, recently consecrated in 1960. We were welcomed by the Bishop himself, Charles Heerey, whose broad Irish accent betrayed his own personal provenance, as that of the Mission itself; paradoxically, an Irish cleric, whose enthusiasm for, and encyclopaedic knowledge of, British royalty drew widespread comment. Our visit had been anticipated; the greetings bestowed upon us by His Eminence, warm but brief. Tony having, as befitted an erstwhile Novice acknowledging a superior Officer of the Church, brushed the Bishop's Ring with his lips. Father Kennedy was accordingly deputed to drive us around town for a spot of sightseeing in the official blue Volkswagen. Tony was keen to execute a research project centring on Catholic Missionary Activity in Onitsha, arranging with the Bishop to pay a return visit in about ten days. Accordingly, without further ado, he was dropped off at the ferry, crossing the Niger, to head directly back to Ibadan, while I opted to hang around for a bit to savour the delights of the seductive wares on offer at the native market. An ebony walking stick with carved head took my fancy and I purchased it, not out of physical necessity, but in deference to an enhanced personal profile which would accompany my public brandishing thereof; still have it. After a bite for lunch, it was off to the ferry across the Niger to Asaba on the western side.

Just sixpence for the half-hour conveyance, in the company of goats, businessmen, beggars, chickens, traders, cheek-by-jowl. In clear view, to the south, we could but marvel at the nigh on completion Niger Bridge, spanning over 4,500 feet. This would be the final piece of the federal jigsaw, the physical symbolic gesture uniting all four of the nation's regions by land. It was scheduled to be formally opened by the Prime Minister himself, Sir Abubakr Tafawa Balewa that coming December, which was to prove his last official government engagement prior to his assassination a month later; the bridge itself destroyed in the Civil War in the 1970s. Meanwhile, jostling on board with the assorted flotsam and jetsam of humanity, of which I was a part, and with the less sentient organic variety of the animal kingdom, as we disembarked on the Asaba side, no hint of an orderly dispersal. I could only suspect that the completion of the fixed span would come as a relief to those forced to suffer this undignified Dante-esque visitation to purgatory on a daily basis. On stepping ashore, it necessitated a climb up the steep muddy track into Asaba. Both sides of the thoroughfare revealed evidence of habitation, by the presence of traditional thatched huts. The outdoor fires were smouldering in an apparent struggle for survival in the face of an intense precipitation visitation, which simultaneously fed rivulets cascading towards the dock from which I had just landed, seemingly determined to raise the water level down below. Feeling pretty jaded, I decided to give Asaba a passing acknowledgement in the course of seeking out the taxi hot-spot, gratefully accepting the offer of one such conveyance and making straight for Benin City, 80 miles further on, where Mr. Omage had arranged with his brother to offer hospitality for the night. Having arrived and located his residence, I discovered to my dismay that the said gentleman was away, and not expected home for another few indeterminate days … But yes, his steward would see to all my requirements. My bed was prepared; on the back of it I began drifting off to the accompaniment of a gathering storm, its intensity rising to alarming proportions, but not before somnolence got the better of me.

The following morning the steward duly aroused me at 7 with a cup of tea, then downstairs for breakfast to a 'full English'; so thoughtful and sensitive to their visitors. I slipped him 10/- in return for his kindness, which actually left me short of readies for the final leg of my return to Ibadan, not least insofar as I wouldn't be going halves with Tony. A visit then downtown to exchange a Traveller's Cheque at Mr. Barclay D.C.O. Nearby the official taxi stand I was accosted by a Yoruba driver who offered to take me the 80 miles or so, for the bargain price of £1:15/-; probably not a licenced operative, given that the law decreed four doors minimum constituted taxi status. It was, nevertheless, a pleasant uneventful journey: no random chickens, just a few long-horned cattle herds to negotiate along the road we had taken a month previously with Mrs. Omage. The by now familiar skyline of Ibadan came into view and I was deposited off the main street close by Leventis. The local bus to the University came by shortly and within 20 minutes I was back on' home territory' as it were at the end of a round trip covering well in excess of 1,250 miles. Up, then, the stone steps to our first floor room in Azikiwe Hall, which had been saved for us for the duration of the vacation, as and when we required it. There was Tony on his bed just waking from his slumber, the heat getting to him. Yet, by sheer good fortune, we had circumnavigated pretty much the multi-faceted organism known as Nigeria by Saturday July 3rd. We had survived this intrepid foray into the unknown, our friendship unsullied.

ON THE OPEN ROAD, PART 2.

For around 10 days we tended to catch our breath in the security of Azikiwe Hall; far fewer folk around, as term had ended. By good fortune the central cafeteria remained open to cater for the skeleton staff and postgrads who had their research to pursue regardless of the constraints of end of term time. Our friend Moses popped in once or twice in between his sporadic visits to Lagos to verify his student status in Nigeria. Tony and I indulged our passion for tennis, having the flexibility to utilise the facilities at a more congenial hour of the day. We read a lot and turned to the BBC Overseas Service in the evenings by means of the little transistor radio I had brought with me. Our subsequent discussions revolved around the current political shenanigans back home. Harold Wilson into his first term as Prime Minister, still in honeymoon mode; just. The Tories, though, in the uncertain prospects of fresh leadership following the departure of Sir Alec Douglas-Home who had led the party to defeat the year previously. It seemed to be a two-horse race in prospect. These front runners, the Veteran Reginald Maudling, a Eurosceptic of his time, was vying with Edward Heath, known for his enthusiasm for seeking to overturn General De Gaulle's veto on our application to join the 'Common Market'. It was all symptomatic at the time of an assessment of Britain's place in the world which our visit to West Africa only served to intensify. British influence on the World Stage was being challenged, post-Imperial syndrome: the continuing tacit acceptance that Apartheid in South Africa was in place for the indefinite future; the unresolved crisis in white ruled Rhodesia unresolved. All such issues provoked scepticism from the leadership of our former colonies in sub-Saharan Africa. 'East of Suez': was this, our proclaimed determination to maintain a meaningful force in the wider world, sustainable diplomatically or even affordable domestically? These considerations went a long way to determine my next option for the remainder of our time in Nigeria: a few days visit to a francophone state would help to secure a more rounded vision of the region. David and Ian had shown up unexpectedly at our door, having had the experience already on their travels in neighbouring Niger; Frank and Andrew then appeared, likewise adding some further national experience to their itinerary beyond Ghana. The neighbouring Republic of Dahomey (now the Republic of Benin) was to be my preferred option: now or never, before we knew it we'd be on the boat for home. Tony had already booked his stay back in Onitsha, so I made tracks.

On Wednesday 14th July, the University had agreed I should travel in the car which was to convey the Vice-Chancellor's wife, Mrs. Dike to Lagos: very generous offer which I had no hesitation in accepting. In Lagos I knew I had a contact, courtesy of the same Mrs. Moore of the Omage connexion. Mrs Adesanya, a Yoruba, had similarly been in Mrs. Moore's class in the U.K. and had subsequently married a prosperous Yoruba lawyer who happened to be a Methodist. Thus sanguine, in the of the distinguished company of K. Onwuka Dike's wife, we duly arrived in Lagos where she alighted at the railway station compound at around 3:30. The driver agreed to drop me off at Kingsway where I partook of poached eggs and a dessert. I'd been given Mrs. Adesanya's address but no phone contact. I took a bus in what I thought was the appropriate direction, to Tinubu Square in the centre, a former slave market, now the site of the imposing Methodist Church to which the Adesanyas belonged. Crossing the Cartier Bridge over the lagoon characteristic of the urban metropolis, an exercise in patience in itself, I alighted at Yaba which featured in the address she had given me. A kind local gentleman, alert to my puzzlement, kindly walked with me to Onike nearby, whereat we tracked down the desired Adesina Street, an unpaved road, but with a row of substantial two-storey dwellings as befitted 'upper middle' success. Presumptuously I knocked on the front door, to be informed by the steward that Mrs. Adesanya was out, but would I like to see Mr. Adesanya? No contest! On explaining the context of my unexpected arrival he invited me to wait for his wife's return from her daily teaching commitments over a freshly brewed pot of tea. On her return, Mrs. Adesanya exhibited delight from receiving the note I had brought for her from Mrs. Moore. Phew! I had crossed the first hurdle. On the basis of that introduction and having explained my purpose of being in Lagos in the first place, I was offered hospitality for the night. We chatted, the three of us, long into the evening over a meal of locally sourced fish, peas, and incongruously 'chips'; perhaps a sensitivity to my own natural palate. Assigned an ensuite bedroom all to myself I gratefully tipped into bed at midnight.

It is difficult to put into words the kindness Mr. and Mrs. Adesanya exhibited towards me. The next morning it was off to school for the good lady. Mr. Adesanya offered me the tour of the city . A lawyer by profession, well proportioned in build, sartorially elegant in dark suit, suave, urbane, but with no hint of affectation, having no set professional engagements for the morning, he was keen to showcase the attractive features of his city. After calling into his Chambers, he drove us by way of the Federal Parliament building, prominent, with a statue of a young Queen Elizabeth II gracing the entrance, on over to Ikoyi Island, the establishment sector: the Mercedes and Bentleys parked in expansive driveways betrayed the residences of those having climbed to Ministerial Status and to Representatives of Missions accredited to the country. Then it was over to Victoria Island Beach, where land was being reclaimed from the sea with the prospect of tourism in mind. It was important to check on transportation to Cotonou. A visit to the Motor Park beckoned and I secured a place on a minibus making the relatively short trip that afternoon. Just time for a meal at the Bristol Hotel: roast pork and with scoops of ice-cream for dessert bolted down in order to make the scheduled departure time back at the terminus, with barely a minute to spare. Despite the unkempt state of the road, and more than one near miss with Dahomeyan vehicles which were still not adjusted to keeping left on crossing the border we made it to the frontier by 3 p.m.

The official national frontier which separates Nigeria from its neighbour, Dahomey/Benin represents the archetypal incongruity thrown up by decisions taken at the Berlin Conference. Both sides of the border, topographically, exhibit the same flat, lagoon coastal based terrain; same rain forest having been extensively cleared in favour of commercial exploitation of oil palm products; for certain, no evidence of a natural divide or delineation. Demographics suggest a self-evident Yoruba ethnicity at this point on either side of the frontier, alongside those of an Aja and Gbe persuasion. Yet the bureaucratic formalities common at all border controls around the world are there to be observed and enforced: passports inspected, visas checked, customs verified: different lingua franca, and driving on the right for starters and a negotiating of economic transactions in a strange currency, the West African Franc.

The very name of the country so called as it was in 1965 betrays the historical legacy of the once powerful kingdom which prevailed in the general area during pre-colonial times. As has been noted, as with all attempts to trace the foundations of West African ethnic groupings, the evidence is clouded by its reliance on oral tradition, distorted by skewed transmission down the centuries. The rise of the Kingdom of Dahomey, as it was at the time of direct French involvement in the area, can be traced back to the Fifteenth Century when its centre of operations was Abomey, inland about 80 miles north of the coast, in the equatorial rain-forest zone, when there is evidence of some form of agreement with the Portuguese even then, to supply slaves. Anxious to relieve itself of its tributary obligations to the Yoruba Empire of Old Oyo of present-day Nigeria (no formal border controls then) an absolute monarchy was established. Further advantage was taken of the presence of the Portuguese at their long-standing foothold at Porto Novo on the then pejoratively termed, globally, as the 'Slave Coast' to accumulate firearms in exchange for slaves in an ever incrementally lucrative enterprise. In essence the kingdom was the more effectively organised for war by its Abomey (a title of the tribal chief as well as the city), Agaja (1708-32). Indeed, Sir Richard Burton's observations of the kingdom referred to its social and political ambience as 'The Black Sparta'.[59] Agaja successfully took control of the coastal operatives of Aliada (1724) and Whydah (1727)[60], unusually employing a feared regiment of female warriors whom the early European contacts referred to as the 'Amazons'. Says a lot about them, doesn't it![61] The distinct ethnicity of the kingdom is characteristically fluid in terms of precise definition: 'Fon' has been asserted as a useful appellation, insofar as they represent a large identifiable demographic component of the modern state. What can be said for certain is that the old kingdom was a conglomerate of clan groupings expanding in common cause in respect of their resentment of, and resistance to, the Yoruba pretentions of Old Oyo. So much for respect due to international boundaries then! As we have seen, Christian Missionary zeal opened up the European exploratory imperative of the early nineteenth century, and with the demands of the Industrial Revolution for a more 'legitimate' trade in tropical resources and expanded markets, so western interests were kindled into competition for controlled access. The Portuguese, who had for so long monopolised the West African contacts, were being sidelined by the more aggressively industrialised nations of the north: Holland, and increasingly the British and the French. France, in particular in the second half of the nineteenth century, was anxious to secure the persona of the Third Republic in the wake of the disastrous humiliation of Napoleon III's 'Second Empire' in 1870-71 at the hands of the new 'Germany' during the Franco-Prussian War. We've already noted its activities in the Senegambia further north up the coast. Interest was now being focussed on the Bight of Benin region where British activities threatened the spheres of influence understanding sealed at Berlin. Ongoing disputes as to the sovereignty of Porto Novo, from which, incidentally, the last Portuguese slave trading ship set sail as late as 1885, long after the British had ended the practice in 1807 as we have seen, led to two fierce Franco/ Dahomean conflicts. The outcome was settled decisively in favour of the French, Behanzin the last Abomey, being deported to the French West Indies, and a formal French Protectorate established in 1894 over what was to become 'French Dahomey' as incorporated into the vast overseas federation of French West Africa in 1904. As expected, the entire conglomerate was an anomalous artificial creation, but subsequently playing an important role in the supply of native troops to the allied cause in the two World Wars of the twentieth century. Administrator Eboue's proclamation from Chad of his pledge to commit French colonial forces in Africa in 1940 to the 'Free French' cause of General de Gaulle played an important role in the North African Desert campaign under the command of General Leclerc the following year. Post-War, in 1946, Dahomey was accorded Overseas Territory status, paving the way for African representation in the metropolitan legislature in Paris, This latter innovation was in direct contrast to the British policy, still wedded in principle to Indirect Rule. The French, in deference to their general sense of pride in their own culture and language, tended to accord honourable status to any 'evoloue', any colonial who embraced and practised francophone identity. Felix Houphouet-Boigny, for example, hailing from the Cote d'Ivoire, just along the way, served as the Minister of Health in Metropolitan France during these post war years. Nevertheless, pressure for Independence mounted, especially since neighbouring Ghana's example in 1957, and the waning interest of France to resist such demands, led ultimately to its being granted in 1960; same year as Nigeria. Politics has tended to follow, and to a large extent emulate, ethnic prejudice as in Nigeria, and with democratic institutions periodically and at times violently undermined. The first President, Hubert Maga, hailed from the northern tribal affiliation until he was overthrown in a military coup in 1963 which was masterminded by Army Officer Soglo who retained power pro- tem until the concession of new elections in 1964. This resulted in the assumption of President Sowon Apithy, whose power base was in Porto Novo, and who was in power when I arrived; yet by December 1965 he himself was the victim of another military coup, this time bloodless: just one month before Nigeria's own bloodthirsty political drama.

Clearing immigration and customs with alacrity, it was a straightforward run to Cotonou. Passing through the capital, Porto Novo, the Assembleé Nationale was prominent in the main square; the same anomaly faced by Nigeria at that time: national legislation emanating from a capital city located on the periphery, at the coast, yet designed to embrace the interests of a populous extending far to the north, over 400 miles distant. The southern rail track ran parallel to the coastal road from hereinon, no barriers hindering access to the permanent way, its open wagon slow moving rolling stock easy game for passengers seeking a profitable, albeit tenuous conveyance. Indian railways spring to mind. Arriving Cotonou at 5:30, it was now a case of seeking the Methodist Mission, my having been given the name of the Superintendent of 'L'Eglise Protestante Methodiste", a Mr. Prickett, who, as per normal would have had no idea I was turning up. The Mission House was ultimately located, after one or two false trails where some smart houses owned by French expats tended to turn out to be red herrings: "Pardon, Monsieur; il n'est pas prés d'ici. Je suis desolee". In the end a young man came up to me, having sensed my dilemma; he knew where it was and escorted me to the Superintendent's residence. On arrival he clapped his hands at the gate, as is the custom in West Africa, to draw attention to visitors to the house. It wasn't Mr. Prickett who emerged in response; on leave apparently. I muttered in English to the gentleman who had come to the door that my unexpected showing up was that "It's a long story", and that Wesley College in Ibadan had given the address as a useful reference point. To my amazement, Rev. Zwaan, a Dutchman as it turned out, his wife and young son, invited me in without hesitation and said I could stay as long as I pleased; couldn't believe my good fortune. A bedroom was prepared, almost as if I was being expected, which comfort I accepted at around 10:30 p.m. after a meal with this charming family. The couple seemed genuinely interested in the circumstances which led to my presence amongst them. My night was spent in profitable sleep, save for one disturbance: the roar of the sound of a passenger aircraft taking off at about 2:30 a.m. The airport runway was at the rear of their compound.

Continental Breakfast with the Zwaan family next morning during which I was apprised of the background to Methodist outreach in Dahomey. The records recount the arrival of one, Rev. Thomas Freeman, from along the coast at Badagri in 1843 who negotiated with 'King Ghezo', a man of substance in the area, and with the latter's blessing, the work started. It was a frustrating beginning on two fronts: the French who at that time had their sights on muscling in on the commercial opportunities of their own, were suspicious of an Anglophone Mission, Protestant moreover. Was this just a covert spying device to subvert their intentions? Secondly, many locals themselves saw it as a potential threat to the practice of 'Vodun' which was prevalent in the area among the Fon. A variation of Obeah, the word Vodun means spirit in the Fon language. Humans are but spirits inhabiting the visible world, who can access the divine reality by communally inducing a trance-like quasi esoteric state of ecstacy, in the course of which superhuman feats can be performed, medical cures effected, advice tendered and 'spells' cast. Like Obeah, the beliefs were tenacious, even after Christianity took on the challenge, bolting on many of its own Platonic, and neo-platonic features of Gnosticism which seem to have a common currency in both. It was a few years later that I recognised the deep-rooted attachment to these arcane performances. On a visit to the francophone Caribbean island of Haiti, the destination to which many Dahomean slaves had been assigned, I was invited to observe objectively one such 'Voodoo' ceremony as it is known there. It was an eye-opener into this world of apparent sprituality.[62] Dare I say it, as I have already hinted, there exists deep in humanity's psyche a quest for what reality is. The question posed by religious sceptics is at least justifiable: Are we not tempted to fashion God in our image, and to bring psychology into play, subconsciously perhaps, to induce hope and 'otherworldliness' in the midst of one's own experience is as a 'slave' to unmitigated misfortune? "There is more in heaven and earth than is dreamed of in your philosophy, O Horatio", reflects the wistful Hamlet as he muses in his own quest for meaning. Maybe the Pentecostal phenomenon of worship amongst the black churches in modern times is a cultural deference to the influences of times past. Be that as it may: the first Methodist chapel on the Dahomean coast was built in 1850, and the faith found concrete expression in Cotonou in 1890, and Porto Novo, 1901. Rev Zwaan's own sense of mission was, I felt, centred around Christ's pronouncement that "inasmuch as you do unto the least of these my brethren, you do it unto me" (Matthew XXV). For Rev Zwaan the gospel has a social imperative, as articulated by David Bown in his book 'Kingdom People',[63] consciously or subconsciously echoing the work and sentiments of Bonhoeffer and the Liberation Theologians of South America who were influencing contemporary progressive Christian thinking at the time.

The Rev and his Mrs. had business to attend to, leaving me to my own devices, free to come and go as I pleased. They lent me a cycle which afforded me flexibility on how I chose to spend the time. It was a profitable excursion out into the town. I followed the tourist trail to all intents and purposes, skirting the vast compound of Apithy's Presidential Palace; a coffee in the restaurant at Monoprix, francophone's version of Kingsway, to write some postcards; to the Post Office to dispatch them, and a spell on the beach, where, as the cooling Atlantic waters lapped beside my bare feet, a young French girl of about 18 came beside me for a chat. Pity I didn't make more of it than I did! Then I checked in at the Bureau de Tourisme, on the basis of which I resolved to head for the 'Venice of Africa', a village on stilts, the following day, within striking distance of Cotonou. I spent the evening engaging with the son of the Rev and Mrs, Zwaan. This little 7 or 8 year old, with more than adequate English at his disposal, his long fair hair necessitating constant tossing of the head to clear the vision of his bright blue eyes, attended a local primary school, seemingly unfazed by the cultural adjustments to which he had been subjected in the face of his parents' vocation. I seem to remember building little tower blocks with him, pre-Lego days; usual game; whose structure could rise the higher before toppling over? Then we poured over a comic book featuring Herge's Tin-Tin, so Belgian, yet produced in the format so beloved and so typically French. He was increasingly at home in the language, more so than I was. What a start the little guy had in assimilating the new culture at grass-roots level, growing up in a multi-cultural setting! Preparation indeed for a progressive post-colonial world. It was to great regret that I later learned, I think at Methodist Mission House in London (as it then was), that the young boy had passed-on in his early teens, the circumstances and details of which were not divulged: tragedy for his delightful parents, and for humanity, for whom the bell tolls.

Presidential Palace, Cotonou, Dahomey.

The next day, being Saturday, my mind was set on a visit to Ganvié, as planned. The village, for all its historic connotations has, like Venice and Brugge (Bruges), the Belgian 'Venice of the North', Ganvié was becoming, as they had become, a bit of a touristic trap; commercialisation was starting to seep in. Accordingly at the taxi park in town I could hire a limo for 560 francs for the afternoon's round trip, 20 minutes each way. Worth it, I thought, given the unique opportunity. The origins of the Ganvié community were the substance of grim reality. Oral tradition recalls that the community was founded on Lake Nokue, in extent 12 miles by 6 miles, by the

Tofino clan grouping as a refuge from rampant Dahomean Kingdom Fon slavers. Dwellings constructed on its northern periphery, the community survived on a diet of fish, and obtaining products of the soil accessed by their wooden dug-out canoes on the mainland when deemed safe to do so. Thus evolved a systematic culture of fish farming, as doubtless encouraged by a Mennonite Christian Mission, whose philosophy is based on pre-industrial simplicity of lifestyle eschewing even mechanical means of transportation. In this regard, it is a focus for overseas visitors, in much the same way that Amerindian 'Reservations' have been synthetically preserved, such as I later experienced at the Caughnawaga settlement outside Montreal: a kind of living museum piece.

Ganvie, Lagoon Settlement, Dahomey

At the dock three or four 'gondoliers' competed for my custom, out of whom I accepted the best offer: the princely sum of 800 francs for 'guaranteed' safe passage. Muscular, short of stature as well as short of banter, he paddled the 8 foot craft with dexterity across what seemed to be a latter day Sea of Galilee, strong wind blowing, but mercifully no need this time for divine supernatural intervention; the assurance of the sustaining presence turned out to be enough. We approached the stilted houses, precariously perched as expected on what seemed to be unstable poles some 10-20 feet above lake level. Within earshot of our approach the inhabitants duly appeared, as if on cue onto their balconies. The smaller children having been trained up, I'm sure, to exhibit their charming best, in order to elicit a 'dash' from the passing trade. Had one weakened to respond, there would be nothing left on which to survive the remainder of the entire trip. In same manner I declined the offer to climb the steps to imbibe at the prominent 'Bar'; the inflated prices on offer would have bled me dry, not to mention my unjustifiable but natural fear at the time that any ensuing lack of judgement consequent on my having one or two might in some way prejudice a safe return to terra firma. It was quite gratifying in a way to see, en route to the dock another tourist being similarly transported in a canoe under similar conditions to my own. It was a relief to land safely whence the hour and a half voyage had started, edified to have added this nautical venture to my store of memories; in many ways the colourful highlight on a brief visit into Dahomey; such was the reflexion on taxi-ing back to my hosts in Cotonou.

It was time to think about making tracks back to Nigeria. Gabriel, a local acquaintance of the Zwaans who had popped round that evening, offered me a lift part way as far as Porto Novo next morning in his Land Rover. Expressing my gratitude to the Zwaans, I took my leave, courtesy of Gabriel where I was dropped off at the long-distance taxi park in the capital. The colonial residue of the French occupation was impressive; Parisian style residences in evidence, French street names with their distinctive calligraphy … and no hint, on the surface at least, of the politically smouldering atmosphere that presaged yet another military coup by the year's end; all very civilised at face value. At the long-distance lorry park, there was not even a mammy wagon destination Nigeria. Taxis there were aplenty, but at 2,500 francs a throw, that option was a non-starter. Nothing for it, then, but to hit the road and take a chance. A lecturer from Dahomey's University stopped and picked me up in his Volkswagen Beetle and kindly dropped me as far as he was going, which as it happened to be pretty much in bush country in the middle of nowhere. Somewhat dispirited, I positioned myself by the side of the road, best thumb forward, when, within a few minutes a white Mercedes with a Nigerian number plate came into view with just the driver visible through the windscreen; must be heading for Lagos. Chance It. To my delight the Yoruba driver stopped. Expressing my gratitude I slid into the leather passenger seat beside him, and was barely into some small talk when, from the rear an imperious voice wafted, behind a shaded glass screen, to the effect, where are you going then? It was quickly established that this was a conveyance at the disposal of a high ranking Nigerian Civil Servant returning from the conduct of official diplomatic business. Stopping for the likes of Me! Mr. Sidi, such was the name he proffered, soon relaxed into friendly conversational mode by the time we crossed the border with the minimum of fuss as befitted the vehicular status; a familiar transient obviously. For the remainder of the journey we engaged in a mutual to and fro-ing exchange ranging from Nigerian history to global politics, punctuated (literally) only by a deflated tyre which the driver resolved with acumen within ten minutes, in the course of which a young girl appeared at the side of the vehicle, with whom Mr, Sidi had a heated conversation about which I remained in total ignorance, it being exchanged in Yoruba. By the time we rolled into Lagos Mr.Sidi and I were on decidedly friendly terms. The car pulled up at the Oudo Hotel in the swank part of town, where Mr Sidi invited me to join him for lunch. On parting, this gracious gentleman slipped a ten bob note into my hand as a contribution towards my bus fare to Ibadan.

On route to the bus terminal, which I located in Iddo, courtesy of the solicitous assistance offered by a member of the local constabulary, I passed the race course. I snatched a clandestine glance through a gap in the fence of the 'Nigerian Derby' being run that day, just as the nags were rounding Tattenham Corner (or the local equivalent). Didn't really raise the level of my adrenaline, not being a punter, and shortly thereafter found the terminus ascertaining that the cream bus 'over there' would be going to Ibadan in "half an hour or so'. At around 5 p.m. in company with an assorted array of passengers, but with plenty of spare space, we drove out onto the highway. Midway, en route, there was the scheduled breather to be had at Shagamu, affording some of the passengers to take the opportunity to replenish their supply of Kola Nuts, this market town being the centre of the distribution of this much prized delicacy. This hard, bitter tasting maroon almond-proportioned aperitif, the product of the trees of the rain forest, had often preceded meal times with our Nigerian hosts; not only as a reputed aid to digestion, but when broken, distributed and shared, a sign and token of spiritual proximity and hospitality; the breaking of the bread at Emmaus (Luke XXIV, 30) occurred to me, and the ongoing presence of our Lord in the celebration of Holy Communion. Shagamu itself has evolved from a conglomeration of Yoruba settlements coming together under the authority of its own Oba, as a defensive feature consequent on the fallout from the decline of the Oyo Empire and associated warfare. Conveniently placed on trade routes from the Niger Delta to the western parts of Nigeria, the town has benefitted from the relatively recently constructed highway directly linking Lagos and Ibadan: a veritable market town.

By 6:45 we had arrived in Ibadan Town Centre; just a matter now to snatch a drink and a bite at the corner convenience buffet abutting the bus terminus, using up the remaining available hard cash on a taxi and back via Mokola, arriving 9:15 at Azikiwe Hall, our apportioned centre of operations. Tony was already ensconced, announcing that Frank and Andrew were around, having decided to make Lagos their departure point together with us, at the beginning of August. It was now July 18th, and our voyage home on the horizon. The ensuing week went by in a flash. Tony and I were able to potter around reading, walking; some tennis, and off on the bus into Ibadan with Andrew and Frank to acquaint them with our, by now, detailed knowledge of the whys and wherefores of a city we'd come to be familiar.

A good idea, I thought to go into Lagos a day early and maybe chance my fortune by inviting myself to stay overnight at the Adesanyas, prior to embarkation on the M.V. Aureol (so named after the hill abutting the harbour in Freetown) on August 3rd. Tony wasn't keen to join me, neither the others, thinking it might well be a bit of an imposition. So, farewell, finally to the University on the 2nd, and luggage in tow, trunk packed off to port, and thence to Lagos by bus. See you tomorrow guys. Don't forget, check in time, 3:30.

Arriving in Lagos by 6 p.m., knowing no shame, I pitched up presumptuously at 7 Adesina Street and the home of the Adesanyas. The steward informed me that Mr. and Mrs. Adesanya were out for the evening, and not expected back until late. The two boys were in, however. They seemed to be at least acquiescent in inviting me in, and in fact the younger of the two, Dayo, aged about 14, quite loquacious, especially when the conversation took on a Beatles focus. A fan, obviously, I feigned more enthusiasm than I felt, being more of a classical man myself. I think I bluffed my way through with sufficient conviction for him to accord me a tacit soul-brother status. We are still in touch to this day, he following in my footsteps by becoming an Ibadan alumnus himself. Time passed until at something to eleven Dayo's parents arrived home, dressed in stunning Yoruba attire, to their surprise encountering me, armed with my abject apologies for this unsolicited intrusion. If there was any hint of irritation on their part, it was masked by an expression of delight that I had come. Furthermore, despite my protestations, Mrs. Adesanya insisted on rattling up a rice-based meal, just for me. They had eaten and the boys had dined earlier. Thing is, I wasn't that hungry, and the enormous dish she placed in front of me only served to intensify my self-loathing. I managed to get through most of it. A bedroom was immaculately prepared for the overnight stay, and it was still with a measure of awkwardness that I slid into the soft furnishings, and so to sleep.

The day of departure dawned. Breakfast having been prepared and served up by the family steward, Mr. Adesanya was prepared to take time out after lunch to deliver me to the Apapa wharf in time for our date with the M.V, Aureol. Earlier he announced that he was going by the hospital to a regular blood donation session; perhaps I would like to join in the process. Again, never having hitherto participated in this worthy enterprise, and with a long sea voyage ahead, I politely passed up the invitation, I shamefully betrayed my Methodist principles; and this, in response to a man who had given up so much of his time for me, and a fellow Methodist to boot! I hasten to add, though, that a year or so later I did sign up as a regular donor, until, that is, a bout of hepatitis contracted in the sub tropics precluded the sacrifice of further pints. At around two Mr. Adesanya deposited me at the wharf, my having duly thanked him for his family's hospitality, I found my five companions already in the passenger lounge, just awaiting the summons to complete the formalities prior to boarding.

A LIFE ON THE OCEAN WAVE, PART 2

Elder Dempster Lines'
AUREOL, built 1951

M.V, Aureol, Lagos to Liverpool

All the documentation having been completed, and checks made by Customs that none of us was attempting to make off with any precious artifacts, we boarded M.V. Aureol, our home for the next couple of weeks. A much sleeker vessel, proportionally, than the Apapa at 538 feet long, 14,000 tonnage, distinctively white in colour, she was the third of the trio employed at the time by Elder Dempster to ply the West Africa run, built in 1951. The 'Apapa', in fact, was a twin of the 'Accra', both having been built a few years earlier in 1948; so the 'Aureol' was the cream of the crop as befitted its livery and known by its aficionados as the 'White Swan'. The ship's routine, we discovered, was very much identical to the format we had followed on the outward voyage, the usual stuff: Bingo, deck cricket, movies, dog racing, the inevitable Carnival Night. Our table for six had been assigned in the First Class Dining Room, our stateroom of similar ilk as before, and all the ancillary appurtenances which make for the cruise. The itinerary had been slightly varied. No stopover at Tema or Banjul; instead we would be docking at Takoradi, Monrovia, with Las Palmas tacked on.

An overnight sailing saw us arrive at Takoradi, an important allied base of operations in World War II, the next morning.[64] (Lawler,N., 'Soldiers, Airmen, Spies And Whisperers: The Gold Coast In World War II'). Like Tema, on the outward journey, this was our Ghanaian port of call, for some reason. Takoradi itself was some 80 or so miles west of Accra, so no time to spend an onshore outing on a second visit to the capital. Prior to disembarkation we were entertained by intrepid enterprising locals diving for coins tossed into the sea by way of their little wooden dinghies alongside the vessel, by passengers from the deck: "it's two bob", they triumphantly exulted, as if in conformation that the feat had been accomplished. On shore, we were able to take advantage of a visit to Elmina Castle, the oldest existing European fortification south of the Sahara, in many ways an illuminative historical pilgrimage evoking poignancy and a fulfilment of our erstwhile landward ventures. Its sturdy stone profile, from a distance, would have withstood comparison alongside any medieval castle built in Europe around 1492, the time of Elmina's construction. Predictably, it was a Portuguese conception, built on firm soil close to the shore. Its 'raison d'etre' of course, was trade with the local chiefly hierarchy, initially for gold extracts, but soon to be supplanted by human trafficking. It has been said of the edifice that "the stark beauty of the whitewashed castle walls contrast deeply with the dark history of this place"[65]. Sums it up really; a stereotypical entrepôt designed to facilitate the transfer of 'property', and as a holding centre for the victims of the pernicious human traffic. There, pretty much in the middle of this imposing structure, itself so designed to showcase Portuguese prestige, was the huge courtyard where the captives were paraded and inspected, deals struck, encapsulating the essence of the whole squalid process. Down the steps, then, from this 'stock exchange' via the spiral stone staircase into the forbidding dungeons, euphemistically described as storage space, in which the unfortunates would have been incarcerated pending the arrival of the sailing vessel destined for the plantations of the 'New World'; such as Samuel Ajayi Crowther and his family would have endured, albeit in Lagos, but it makes no difference, before his fortuitous release at the hands of the Royal Navy. The fort itself, captured by the Dutch in 1637, Elmina continued to bear witness to the barbarous practice for another 250 years or more. In 1872 the fort was ceded to the British, wherein its facilities were adapted for use to 'house' prisoners taken during the Ashanti wars of the period, reference to which has already been made. As with most of the European colonisation along the west coast and beyond, it was these toeholds which formed the springboard for formal occupation and sovereignty after 'Berlin'. In this case, the colony of the Gold Coast, as pre-independent Ghana had been known. Our short minibus journey back to the vessel was a sombre reflexion on the inhumanity of the past, to which we are the heirs, and further where much work still needed to be done. This, after all, was the era of Martin Luther King 'over the other side'; his 'Dream' speech of the previous August almost 12 months to the day, the Civil Rights Movement; ongoing repercussions right down to the present, when 'Black Lives Matter. In many ways, the inheritance of what is symbolised by Elmina.

Elmina Castle, Ghana

Interestingly and paradoxically, our next landfall was to be Monrovia, at two days' voyaging distance: the American equivalent of Freetown. Like Freetown, just along the coast, this subsequent capital city of Liberia, appropriately so named, the settlement was founded in the 1820s. Sponsored at the behest of the 'African Colonisation Society' based in the U.S.A., it had been named in honour of its fifth President, James Monroe (1821-25), he of the 'Monroe Doctrine' with its anti-Imperialist overtones. The national flag of the territory has borne all the hallmarks of U.S. provenance; never mind the fact that George Washington himself had been a Virginian slave owner. In many respects, Monrovia became a mirror image of Freetown, as its authority expanded into the hinterland, the demand for rubber derivatives as resourced from the interior, as the nineteenth century rolled on, pejoratively branded the country as the neo-colonial 'Firestone Republic'. Like Sierra Leone, there were the inevitable tensions arising between the 'imported' liberated slaves and the indigenous clan groupings of the interior: the largely Islamic Mandingo-apeaking Malinke, the Kru and Grebo who were subsequently counted among the first Christian converts in the country. Formal independence was proclaimed in 1847, with James Roberts sworn in as the first president of the first black republic in Africa; the only state never having been formally and politically subject to colonial rule. Abyssinia (the modern Ethiopia) could certainly claim similar status; its history, however has been tarnished by Mussolini's grab of the territory in 1935 until liberation towards the close of World War Two. Liberia's 1847 Constitution was modelled on that of the U.S.A., shorn of its Federal features: Executive President, law framing Legislature, and Independent Judiciary. Some modification to the structure in latter days, and the tendency for some presidents to overstep their executive authority. Nevertheless, the Constitution has effectively remained in place, surviving the Civil War of the 1990s, and the election of Ellen Sirleaf Johnson as the first female President in Africa (2006-18).[66] At the time of our visit, the presidency was held by William Tubman, having held office continuously since 1944 until his death in 1971. With staunch Methodist credentials, wide-scale reforms are credited to him: the breaking of the elitism which had characterised the Monrovia political establishment, the upgrading of educational opportunities and the practical recognition of the inclusivity of the indigenous tribal groupings of the interior: to the point whereby the capital recorded the majority of its natural indigenous inhabitants being in the majority. Nevertheless, Tubman's long tenure had been inevitably attributed to, and tainted with, accusations of an authoritarian paternalistic approach. In 1961 Monrovia had been established as the first Headquarters of the Organisation of African Unity, in deference to its tradition of sustained independence.

Monrovia, Beachscape, August 6ᵗʰ 1965

Unfortunately, due to a quick turn-around, our shore-time was limited to about an hour, and short circuited to the port area. However we glimpsed from a distance the edifice of the recently erected Capitol building, echoing its Washington counterpart, erected in 1958. Similarly, Tubman's Executive Mansion was spotted, and that's about all, unfortunately, given the unique history associated with this English speaking republic, since sadly ravished by the spectre of Civil strife.[67]

A revisiting of Freetown was scheduled on Saturday 7th August after overnighting on board; again we were in for something of a surprise; no landing for us at all; disappointed of course, but we had had the satisfaction of exploration on the outward leg. The reason for this restriction was soon to become apparent. At the quayside, as we docked, a mass band, military style, in pukka formation, was lined up ready for action in front of the gangway onto the vessel. In due course an official saloon drew up alongside, emerging from which the personage we recognised as Sierra Leone's Prime Minister, Sir Albert Margai. The Honour Guard snapped to attention, but the band remained muted. Minutes later a limousine bearing all the hallmarks of an even more distinguished dignitary, a crown boldly emblazoned front and rear. As the door opened to reveal the identity, the National Anthem struck up, and an Honour Guard escorted the Governor-General onto, and up the gangway, with Prime Minister in tow. It was, in fact, His Excellency Sir Henry Lightfoot Boston, representative of Her Majesty the Queen in the territory; and he was travelling on 'our' ship in the course of his duties. As Governor- General of an independent nation his duties were largely titular and ceremonial, bur honorific just the same. Doubtless he would dine with the Captain at top-table and be accorded the finest stateroom on board as indeed was to be the case. Having bade farewell to the G-G, Sir Albert quipped to the captain that one day he "would like a ride in your boat". Sir Albert had, in fact, succeeded his brother, Sir Milton Margai, the 'Father of the Nation', on the death of the latter the year previous. The brothers had hailed from a chieftain family in the indigenous region of Banta, unlike Sir Henry who was of Freetown Creole stock. Each of them highly educated in either the medical and legal fields, they had steered the country gently into independence by means of the Sierra Leone People's Party with which the Margais had been long associated. They had skilfully won the confidence of both the creole element, as well as the indigenous populous to secure the requisite majority in the legislature. The civic role having been played by Sir Henry, was rewarded with the technically non-partisan office he now held. Little hint at the time of the devastating Civil War which was to engulf the country and Liberia for several years as the century moved on.[68]

Sir Albert Margai, Prime Minister of Sierra Leone, disembarking the M.V. Aureol having paid a courtesy call on H.E, Sir Henry Lightfoot Boston's departure for a visit to the U.K., August 7th 1965.

Still on board then, we had the prospect of three clear days before our next scheduled landfall. Again it was all predictable diversions to keep one amused. Captain's Divine Service in the first Class Lounge at 11 on the Sunday, followed by the Captain's Cocktail Party in the Smoke-Room at 12:30. Cricket Match, Passengers v Crew in the afternoon. I performed right-handed so as to 'give the others a chance'; such was my reputation on the evidence of the outward voyage. The Musical Recital featured recordings of Mantovani and his Orchestra playing such favourites as The Dream of Olwen, The Cornish Rhapsody and The Warsaw Concerto to round off the day after evening meal. Cinema presentations were ongoing, featuring The Ipcress File, Topkapi, and The Seventh Dawn. Carnival Night lived up to its propensity for revelry; even the G-G on top table donning a paper hat, and joining in with gusto, inviting one of my friend's (won't say which) less than judicious observations that the G-G staggered out "in a drunken stupor". As for me, no cigars this time: lessons had been learned.

Our final port of call was to be Las Palmas, on the island of Gran Canaria, one of the Canary Islands archipelago. Hardly Africa, in the eyes of today, but I suppose on the continental shelf, akin to the Falkland Islands and Argentina. There are, nevertheless, historical demographic links to bolster their claim to African identity. Arab traders were known to have an interest in doing business there, by the turn of the first millennium, perhaps with the Guanche people who were reputedly of Berber extraction, and who themselves, therefore, must have originated on the African mainland. At some point the Guanche could well have kayaked the 60 odd nautical miles in search of greener pastures on the islands, leaving behind the more tenuous existence on offer in the Sahara. It was they whom the Spanish finally subdued and assimilated during the Fifteenth Century. Its mountainous volcanic topography has left richly endowed residue on which oranges, sugar cane, dates, coffee, bananas, tomatoes and tobacco have at one time or another thrived. The islands were visited, post-High Renaissance by Genoese, French and of course, goes without saying, the inevitable Portuguese. Columbus replenished his small armada of vessels on his historic voyage of discovery in 1492; subsequently the islands became a regular and scheduled refuelling watering hole for Spanish enterprise in the New World. To secure this benefit the Treaty of Alacovas was signed in 1496 which recognised Spanish sovereignty over the archipelago.[69] It was from here that Generalissimo Francisco Franco launched his initial Nationalist revolt against the Spanish Republic in 1936, aiming to hit the mainland proper via Spanish Morocco.[70] Post-war, of course, the islands have evolved into a favoured destination for northern European tourists, in search of an equable sub-tropical climate, blue seas, sandy beaches, and within striking distance. Our own visit on Wednesday the 11th was underwhelming. We'd seen seaside resorts before, back home: same tacky amusement arcades, swish hotels and modest guest houses, albeit with weather less favourably guaranteed; Europeans even sweeping the streets. Hence our morning was somewhat aimless, and we ambled back to the wharf to board the Aureol for the last time.

Overlooking Las Palmas, Canary Islands, 1965

The home strait now; four days without landfall and the Bay of Biscay in prospect. As it turned out, Poseidon was content to deal gently with us this time by the provision of a benign tidal swell, rather than the violent rage which he had forced us to endure on the outward stretch. Perhaps Neptune felt that we'd experienced enough excitement already. On board there was the Thursday evening 'Race Meeting' to distract us; the Farewell Dinner and Dance to endure on the Saturday. Either there was no suitable or available lady amongst the ex-Colonial types or the wives of Mende Chiefs on board with which to display our collective public exhibition on the floor (where we would probably end up anyway), or we were just shy. Whatever, we beat a hasty retreat to our respective billets as soon as diplomacy would permit. The Sunday at 11 was the Captain's Divine Service in the First Class Lounge a la the 'Apapa', this time in thanksgiving for a potentially safe return. Never has 'Eternal Father, strong to save' been so meaningfully belted out! Shortly thereafter, in the course of a nostalgic stroll on deck, I chanced upon the G-G, sober by this time. As a kind of memento I took the liberty of asking him for his autograph, to which he graciously acceded, in the flyleaf of my copy of Christopher Fyfe's 'A History of Sierra Leone' which I happened to have on my person at the time. Our verbal exchange was otherwise limited and very much to the point, his only remark being what was clearly uppermost on his mind: his take on the climate: "It's so cold", as he took his leave with the briefest of pleasantries to continue his solitary perambulation, as I did with mine.

By first light on Monday 16th August we were up and last minute packing. On deck, despite a sea mist, we ascertained we were northbound up the Irish Sea, coast of Wales to starboard, Ireland to port, Isle of Man somewhere in between; Liverpool imminent. Our venture to the West Coast helped focus our minds on the port to which we were about to enter; yes, the city which nurtured The Beatles, the 'Ferry cross the Mersey'; the home of the Soccer Reds. But its dark history could no longer be ignored. As the Slave Trade capital of Europe during the late Eighteenth Century having replaced both London and Bristol in the numbers transported, its street names, statues of 'benefactors', the Port Building itself, all resonate with the blood of well over a million human lives transported from the coast from which we had just come. The merchants who enriched themselves on the evil of such commerce and who have for so long been eulogised for their philanthropy in respect of their fellow citizens are now posthumously being called to account for the provenance of their largesse. The city, which grew filthy rich on the importation of slave-grown cotton on the back of the erstwhile Triangular Trade, the city whose patricians backed Jefferson Davis and the Confederate States in America to win, still bears material witness to its regrettable Victorian legacy. Thoroughfares such as Rodney Street, Tarleton Street, even Penny Lane, testify to men of prominence associated with such ill-gotten gains. Even the family of the liberal, evangelical Prime Minister, W.E. Gladstone, has been overtly implicated, and whose public image has thus been tarnished.[71] It was into these very docks that a much chastened John Newton returned to take up a more benign functionary role prior to his ordination as Vicar of Olney. With these musings exacting a toll on my complacency, it was, nevertheless down to breakfast, with our first perusal of English Newspapers for months. Without much thought I grabbed the first available. Happened to be the 'Daily Express' at which some ex-Colonial at the next table made a barely disguised derogatory remark at my choice. Then he apologised with the hint of a smile: "Been on the West Coast too long!" as if that explained everything. Off the vessel by 10:30, allowing Sir Henry to set the tone, although he was nodded through Customs and Immigration with formal alacrity, whereas we had the full monty of bureaucracy with which to contend.

Approaching Liverpool Waterfront from the Sea, 1965

The formalities concluded, farewell Aureol, farewell Elder Dempster, we emerged into the waiting area where the parents of one of the six had journeyed up to Liverpool for an advance reunion, to unabashed delight. A light lunch in their company, souvenirs exhibited, we set off for the designated 'Boat Train' (still had them in those days!) which was to convey us to Euston; uneventfully anti-climatic as it turned out, as we traversed England's green and pleasant land. 'And was Jerusalem builded here?' Heaven is where, at root, the heart yearns to be, and that means finding its natural home. It's as much the case for the nomadic Tuareg pastoralist raised in the Sahara, the Amerindian at one with nature on the Great Plains, as it's expressed in the African inspired soul music of the American South, the Caribbean rap, as it is for Tony's roots in the extremity of his native Cornwallian St. Ives.

Euston: Frank's girlfriend, now his wife, waiting faithfully for him on the platform; our assorted respective relatives; my Dad.

SOAS in September guys!

POSTSCRIPT

This account began with the basic premise that decisions brokered at the Berlin Conference 1884-85 bedevilled a systematically logical evolution of West African society under what ought to have been an orderly albeit gradual transition to independence. Thus when we arrived in April 1965 the countries were basking uneasily in the first flush of nationhood. The Gambia just two months in was in the throes of recent celebrations marking the event. For the time being, Sierra Leone, four years on, Nigeria after five, and Ghana since 1957, the Anglophone nations, still retained a semblance of stability, with their respective ruling cliques to whom power had been originally entrusted, keeping the lid on underlying tensions.

Less than six months after our return to the U.K., Nigeria's tragedy unfolded. The strain of holding together a Balkanised Federation cobbled together in an attempt to woo the disparate populous by means of sanguine compromise gave way on January 15th, 1966.[72] A cabal of Army Officers conspired to wreak revenge on what they saw as a Northern dominated oligarchy, aided and abetted by quisling southern politicians in their own opportunistic lust for power. Sir Ahmadu Bello, the Sardauna of Sokoto and Premier of the Northern Region was assassinated in Kaduna; S.L.Akintola, the errant Yoruba Premier of the Western Region, life cut short in Ibadan. Most distressing of all, Sir Abubakr Tafawa Balewa, Federal Prime Minister, gone missing, abducted, whose body was subsequently to be discovered cast into a ditch outside Lagos. A day version of the 'Night of the Long Knives'. Citing corruption, mismanagement and inefficiency for this drastic turn of events, its Igbo inspired and executed coup d'etat could scarcely conceal the fact that it was a southern reaction to northern dominance. The more so, since General Ironsi, himself an Igbo, having successfully quelled the rebellion, seized power, and proclaimed himself Head of State. Within a year he too was dead, the victim of a counter-coup of northern army officers, bringing Lt. Colonel Gowon to office, indirectly provoking the pogroms against Igbos in the north, accounting for the vengeful deaths of hundreds: in itself, to presage the destructive Biafran Civil War whose catalyst, Colonel Ojukuwu, sought to detatch the former Eastern Region from the rest of the country in 1967. The conclusion of the bitter long-drawn out struggle in favour of a politically reunited nation in 1970, has never fully brought an end to the bitter enmities which have so blighted the nation. The return of Civilian Rule by the turn of the millennium has done little to heal the wounds, The rise of Boko Haram in the North-East, the misguided violence in its misguided abuse of Q'uranic scriptures 'justifying' its determination to impose Sharia Law on the northern states, has brought untold misery to thousands. Boko Haram's avowed links to ISIS and the attempt to establish an Islamic state has done nothing to foster a common purpose for Nigeria. The abduction of some 300 girls from their largely Christian school in Chibok during 2014 has been but one of the extreme measures the group has taken to pursue its pernicious ends; all unresolved to this day, despite the efforts of Britain, the former colonial power, to aid the official Nigerian Government of former President Goodluck Jonathan, and present incumbent Muhammad Buhari. Other such villages in Kaduna State have been especially vulnerable to this ongoing violence. Such persecution of Christians, in the North, can be seen, in part, as the reaction towards the 'white' religion of the imperialist powers and its perceived historical subordination of Islam; again, an indirect long-term consequence of the Berlin Conference, and the cobbling together of the hybrid Nigerian nation.

The old federal regions have long since gone, replaced by smaller 'states' 30 plus in number, with at least nominal powers, the more effectively as a sop to the smaller indigenous groupings in their quest for recognition. Even so, many Igbos in particular still look back nostalgically to the dream of an independent Biafra. Lagos has been sensibly replaced as the nation's capital by Abuja, a modern purpose built city in the centre of the country. Sterling has been replaced by the Naira as the national currency. An effort has been made to improve the highway structure financed in large measure by the oil boom of the 1970s; right-hand drive has been introduced to align its system to the neighbouring francophone states, despite its comforting continued commitment to Commonwealth membership which acts as a global perspective on some form of national introspection. Nevertheless, what transpired at Berlin makes the experience of Nigeria the quintessential victim of the decisions taken there in 1884-85. As Sir Hugh Clifford, a pre-war Governor of the country, described 'Nigeria' as a "collection of independent nation states separated from one another by great distances, different … in ethnological, racial, tribal. political, social and religious barriers". Just about sums it up really.

The experience of neighbouring Ghana initially followed in Nigeria's footsteps: the architect of its independence, and in many ways the doyen of modern African nationalism, Kwame Nkrumah, was toppled in 1966, again by military coup and heralding a period of military rule down to 1989. Justifiable criticism of his increasingly messianic presumption and corrupt tendences have been cited as reasons for his downfall. Wordsworth's "Blest was it in that dawn to be alive, But to be young was very Heaven"[73] was, for better or worse, the sentiments of numerous students on the street on hearing the news. Nevertheless, being substantially smaller than Nigeria and less traditionally diverse, Ghana's internal problems have been correspondingly less acute. The military dictatorship of the charismatic Jerry Rawlings, which paved the way to his assumption of elected authority, did much to restore some faith in the Liberal Democratic format during his tenure from 1981 to 2001. Ghana's contribution to Commonwealth membership is valued, and its present Head of State, President Nana Akufo-Addo is heir to this inheritance.

Despite its initial encouraging launch into independence under the Margai brothers, the accession to the leadership of Siaka Stevens, in 1967, and a short interlude of military rule under Brigadier Juxon-Smith, gave rise to the abusive exploitation of the country's diamond resources: illicit deals, corrupt influence and smuggling, from which the government itself cannot be exonerated. Stepping down in favour of a quasi hand-picked successor, Stevens handed the reins of executive power to President Mamoh, himself not immune to the accusation of blatant corruption in 1985. This, coupled with his disastrously inept mismanagement of the Economy led to the creation of a guerrilla style armed challenge to his government, aided and abetted by neighbouring Liberia's Charles Taylor's National Patriotic Front which was intervening to engineer Mamoh's overthrow. The Civil War which ensued, 1991-2001 was bitter, and exacerbated by the extensive use of child warriors and the exchange of 'blood diamonds' at the coast in exchange for weaponry which of course only protracted the struggle.[74] All that can be said is that, in Sierra Leone's favour at this time, it was not ethnic rivalry which precipitated the conflict; it was the corruption and resultant disparity of wealth distribution which led to the disaffection with the peaceful democratic process. So blatant was the abuse of children during this cross-border conflict that only armed peace-keeping missions sponsored by the United Nations and with strident active intervention from Tony Blair's Britain eventually brought the war to an end.[75] In 1992 leadership was passed to President Strasser who toppled Mamoh in a military coup, becoming the world's youngest Head of State at the tender age of 25 until ousted by his erstwhile deputy, President Bio, who subsequently held office as head of a military junta for a matter of months. He is currently President of the nation, elected in 2018, parliamentary democracy having been restored; the prospects now look relatively optimistic.

The Gambia, which had been our first footfall on the outward journey, has had, by comparison, a more settled time of it since 1965. Sir Dawda Jawara, the architect of independence, soldiered on as leader of this anomalous entity, surviving a military coup in 1981 with the material aid supplied by neighbouring Senegal. The price of this assistance was the formation of a confederation of the two countries as Senegambia whereby resources and infrastructure could be 'shared'. This lasted down to 1988, when incompatibility between the legacy left by the departing colonial powers proved its undoing. Ultimately Jawara was overthrown in a bloodless coup in 1994 by Yahya Jammeh. He presided over a military dictatorship, until being constitutionally elected as President in 1996.

During 2013 Jammeh suddenly announced the unusual step of withdrawing from the Commonwealth, as he saw it a colonial relic with no place in modern Africa. By so doing the country lost its place in the great comity of global nations who continue to pool their knowledge based on a common heritage of British influence, a common language, legal system; a further forum at which nations can air their views informally in the atmosphere of a non-threatening family get together, recognising that the monarchy plays an important symbolic unifying role, and a quadriannual celebration of the Commonwealth Games. Hence Jammeh's unprecedented announcement; the more so, given his reasons, that non-Anglophone African nations who had never had previous constitutional links with the U.K. were queueing up to join: Cameroons, Mozambique and Rwanda. In the 2017 General Election Jammeh initially refused to concede defeat, despite having lost to Adama Barrow in the General Election. The upshot was that Barrow was sworn in at the Embassy in neighbouring Senegal, and as such became the legal Head of State. In 2018 the country's application to rejoin the Commonwealth was accepted. As of 2020 there seems to be some form of equilibrium restored.

Mention has already been made of the ups and downs of Dahomey/Benin post 1965; the Civil War in Liberia on the passing of William Tubman[76]. A colonial style war was still being fought in Portuguese Guinea, and trouble brewing in Spain's possession of the Rio de Oro. All, fortunately now resolved, or at least patched up. The conclusion must be drawn, therefore, that the European 'Scramble for Africa' was symptomatic of a quick fix to settle scores from a European perspective in 1884-85.[77] No real consideration was given to the long-term problems arising from the arbitrary drawing of boundaries in respect of indigenous interests, the resultant need to hold the simmering tensions in check during colonial rule, and the explosive uncorking of the unstable contents of the bottle once it had been removed. Sir Hugh Clifford's comment was indeed prescient.

The regular sea-going passenger facility between Liverpool and Lagos has long since gone. The Apapa was withdrawn from service in 1968, and the Accra at about the same time, leaving the Aureol as the sole remaining vessel on the run until its own final voyage in 1974. The 'White Swan' survived for a bit in other guises, based overseas, until ending her days in a breakers' yard on the Indian sub-continent. The residue of the old colonial clientele had by that time virtually dried up, and of course airlines had taken over as the preferred conduit between the West Coast and Europe. Elder Dempster itself soldiered on in name for a few more years, chiefly as a cargo line, but the company was finally wound up in 2000, but still fresh in the memories of those still around who were its lifeblood.

- A debt of gratitude must be reiterated to SOAS, and to Roland Oliver in particular, for the visionary enterprise which made such a visit possible. It transformed our world view, and hopefully informed the path our lives were to take for the better. At the very least, stereotypical images were refashioned. It induced a more philosophical perspective in terms of our take on how we viewed people who were not familiar. This all seems very commonplace now, but in the mid-Sixties this was something of a breakthrough in our thinking. The common thread of humanity, in all its diversity, reveals the unspoken yearning for humankind to determine greater meaning. The need to explain reality by means of creation stories, as passed down by diverse ethnic groupings all strike a similar chord: the Oduduwa 'architectural' concept of the Yoruba, the chi 'soul possession' to explain the conscience element in Igbo folklore, as is explored with such clarity in Chigozie Obioma's recent novel 'An Orchestra of Minorities'. The Hausa/Fulani devotion to the example set by holy people of the past, is common to those faiths of the Abramic tradition, wbich just happens to tie in with the yearnings of the Hebrew of the 40 Years wandering in the Desert[78], and that of the Christian quest for the reality beneath the shadows in sharing the 40 days in the Wilderness[79] in an echo of Platonic revelation[80]. John Hick's concept of the unity in diversity as explored in his cosmological 'Copernican Revolution' whereby all honestly interpreted revealed faiths as received in their respective cultural and geographical contexts has great appeal: as the reality of the light of the sun informs each planet with different intensity and perception, so the great unfathomable mind who chose to design a Universe out of love for architecture is limited not by its own power and strength, but by the cultural circumstantial perception by which each community, each individual receives it[81]. Yet, as Obioma and Achebe, those contemporary Nigerian novelists of distinction have laid bare, such beliefs can be served up by opportunists, with their own perverse agenda, as catalysts for division, differentiation and worse. The frailty of human nature to exploit 'otherness' spuriously for the purpose of asserting one's own self-worth is one of our besetting sins. In the words of Achebe, others have had, and still have, the potential to "put a knife in the things that held us together and we have fallen apart". The Africa which we six witnessed in the Sixties has all the hallmarks of this historical evidence of humanity's propensity for intolerance and weakness: not just that of one so-called ethnic classification, but of an opportunity to recognise the collective responsibility of all of us blessed as we all are with the privilege and capacity of rational thought; such as that which has allowed primitive emotional needs to attempt to erect a Tower of Babel. As Obioma reminds us, "Pride erects a wall around a (person's) inner-self", but the consequent thoughtless fruit can so easily morph into the "shame (which) pierces that wall and strikes (that) inner self in the heart".

- "Black Lives Matter" is the buzz in 2020, a phrase that would not have seen out of place coming from the eighteenth century lips of Olaudah Equiano[81a] The tragically callous violence perpetrated against George Floyd in Minneapolis has triggered an outpouring of global protest and rightly so. It is appropriate that all forms of injustice and negative discrimination are publicly and dramatically articulated. The cause for which the protesters are advancing is indeed a noble one. We must take care, nevertheless, that the slogan itself avoid running the risk of exacerbating prejudice and inviting a perverse right-wing backlash. At a time when globally all are susceptible, at the time of writing, to Covid 19, we are reminded of our common humanity, and with it of our responsibility to our neighbour whoever she or he might be. In some ways, it could be argued, "All Lives Matter" is the alternative slogan behind which all should be marching, to focus additionally upon the inherent vulnerability of the LGBT community, and indeed those of the female gender, in the wake of the recent high profile tragedy of Sarah Everard. One might even go further: it could imply, if one so wishes, to embrace the innocent lives of the yet unborn; they who have had not the opportunity, even, to express their views, let alone march of their own volition. To many, such a banner encompassing "All", by its very nature, is inclusive. it is less intimidating, less aggressively provocative, yet embracing and extolling the very same principles. David Olusoga makes this point clearly in his current BBC production in the series 'Black and British: A Forgotten History'. The Trans-Atlantic Slave Trade was an evil blot on the human catalogue of collective crime. Slavery, its aftermath and the evolution of Capitalism, as Eric Williams argues, certainly paved the way for its institutional acceptance at the time[82]. The Slave Trade and Slavery itself bred the endemic racial stereotyping, discrimination and segregation, long after its formal abolition: in the U.S.A., southern Africa, the Caribbean, and in a global context more generally. Yet, the sheer barbarism of its practice was only empowered by the complicity, at least initially, of the indigenous agencies of authority, whose equally callous disregard for 'their own' made it possible. This binary complicity between white capitalist entrepreneurs and indigenous 'chiefs' has been acknowledged by Nigerian journalist and novelist Adeobi Tricia Nwaubani in her recent BBC communication[82a]. She quotes A. E. Afigbo whose research revealed that 'the (British colonial) government was aware of the fact that the coastal chiefs and the major coastal traders had continued to buy slaves from the interior into the 20th Century', discretely tolerated as such on political and economic grounds[82b]. Her great-grandfather, Chief Ogogo was one such, who was in many ways a magnanimous benefactor, but who nevertheless willingly traded internally in human trafficking. "Assessing the people of Africa's past by today's standards would compel us to cast the majority of our heroes as villains". By the same token, the portrait of George

Washington, a Virginian slave owner, on the American dollar bill could be cited as a suitable candidate for replacement. After all, let's not forget that Al Capone exploited 'his own' in order to profit from the institutional constraints of the Prohibition era. White, Black, whatever, each of us shares, by implication, albeit accepted in the context of its time, in the collective responsibility for this lamentable outrage against humanity, one amongst the many and various evils which have blighted our historical narrative.

• This concept was fully brought home to us on our trip, as we were the recipients of supreme human kindness, in the process of which we were witnesses of the huge injustices which have been perpetrated by those of all hues; of those of us who are prepared to grab any selfish advantage which circumstances have thrown in our path. We six ourselves did precious little to deserve the good fortune to have been born as and when we were; neither did Bishop Samuel Ajayi Crowther; neither did the little guy with elephantitis whom I encountered begging on the station at Kafanchan; nor did the 'deck passengers' exposed to the heat on our passage from Banjul to Lagos deserve their lack of it, while we luxuriated in the solicitous regard paid to us as the fortunate clients of Elder Dempster. Did we ourselves, on our travels, not, albeit sub-consciously, trade on our obvious veneer of expatriana, turning up as we did 'on spec' at random locations, sometimes around midnight, on the assumption we would be accepted without question, as indeed we were?

• Blame 'Berlin' as a root cause of the misfortunes of present-day West Africa is that to which this analysis points, and the premise on which the synthesis is based. Yet 'Berlin' is but a symptom of the greater malaise to which we as a common humanity is prone: "Let (the one) who is without sin cast the first stone"[83]. That fateful Berlin Conference itself was but a reaction to what had gone before, and as such the 'blame' can be traced back almost to infinity. One of my respected colleagues of African ancestry at H. O. Nash High School in Nassau, Bahamas, a teacher of some repute, remarked how he acknowledged positively, albeit with a hint of guilt, that his ancestor had actually become the victim of the Slave Trade; otherwise he, my colleague, probably wouldn't have reaped the benefits of the educational opportunities the 20th Century Caribbean offered; statistically, my colleague's chances are implicitly more likely to be as the victim of ebola, malaria, aids, yellow fever, poverty, had he been raised in contemporary Africa: a view, blunt such as this, lacking in overt sensitivity towards the blatant evil of the historical human traffic, and to the monumental struggles which the African people have been forced to confront in light of the imperial legacy. Nevertheless, in the wider universal context, sentiments worthy of some thought. "Bloom where you are planted", is incumbent upon us all, in order to give practical expression to the idea that humanity is created in the image of the Great Architect of the Universe[84], whoever one is, and wherever the location or quality of the soil by which we are nurtured.

• Our 'Tropical Trip' in 1965 opened our eyes to something of these important truths. Whether or not we have lived up to the privileges to which we, collectively or individually, were exposed only history will judge. Whatever, Thank you to our hosts at the Universities of Ibadan, Ife and Ghana for the kindness we received; to those with whom we relied for accommodation and hospitality; Thank you, SOAS.

Where Since?:

Andrew Crozier: distinguished in academia; author and lecturer in History, Queen Mary College, University of London, University of Bangor, New York University.

Frank Curry: the only one of us to graduate' First Class Honours'; subsequently a member of the British Antarctic Survey and Logistics/Operations Officer. Ministry of Defence.

David Hedges: academia; latterly supervisor of post-graduate studies at the University of Mozambique, Maputo.

Ian Piper: a socially focused career: The International Red Cross, Geneva; The European Commission, Brussels; The BBC World Service, London.

Tony McWilliams: Post-grad at University of Makerere, Uganda; teacher and Civil Servant.

John Berryman: Post-grad, Oxford & USA; teacher, Caribbean and Bede's, Sussex.

The Apapa Six: Reunion, London, Spring 2015
L to R: Andrew, Ian, Writer, Tony, Frank, David

ACKNOWLEDGEMENTS

This Journal owes its genesis to the History Dept. faculty at SOAS under its visionary pioneer, Professor Roland Oliver. He engineered an experience which was life affirming and gratitude for the opportunity is well overdue. The equivalent depts in the Universities to which we were attached: Legon, Ife, and Ibadan made our stay memorable for which we are sincerely thankful. Those good folk who offered hospitality during our travels, often when we showed up without prior warning: the Adesanya family in Lagos, the Omages in Benin City, the Zwaan family of Cotonou, Tom Wells at Kano, Tony Kirk-Greene in Zaria and Rev and Mrs. Johnson's kindness in Kaduna. These and many more went the extra mile to accommodate our venture.

The account of these experiences owes much to the encouragement of the publishing staff at Balboa Press, notably Donald Stephens and May Arado who have seen me through the inadequacies of my I.T. skills. Their patience has been invaluable.

Closer to home I have been supported by friends who have read the scripts and offered Sage advice: authors in their own right, David Bown, Simon Morgan and his wife Karen. Sir Bob Russell, my cousin and erstwhile M.P. for Colchester has, from a distance, kept me upbeat throughout by means of his regular words of affirmation on an almost daily basis. The friendship of my colleagues at Bede's School have been a constant source of inspiration as have my students over the years. To Roger and Angela Perrin I owe a particular debt. The Adebisi family of Ibadan: Edward, Michelle and their children Jason, Natasha, Laura and Jay are an inspiration to the human Spirit: at home in their Marella School in Nigeria, as much as at Bede's School in the U.K. Their Unseen encouragement is incalculable. My wife Isabelle has helped with the I.T. dimension inherent in a production such as this. I'm particularly grateful to my children, Livingston and Anouk for their contribution to some of the artwork. The family has borne the brunt of my shortcomings occasioned by the time spent away from domestic duties as this project unfolded. Finally, the incomparable friendship of the Apapa 6 which has been sustained so faithfully over half a century is what has given legs to this testimony. Love you all.

John Berryman, February 2021, Battle, Sussex.

REFERENCES

1 Cowden, J.E., 'Elder Dempster Fleet History, 1852-1985)'.

2 Perrin, R.A., 'Why Does Anyone Want To Go To Your School?'.

3 Uzoigwe, G., 'Britain And The Conquest of Africa: The Age Of Salisbury'.

4 Hochschild, A., 'King Leopold's Ghost: A Story of Greed, Terror, and Heroism in Colonial Africa'.

5 Lugard, F., 'The Dual Mandate in British Tropical Africa'.

6 Nijman, J., Muller, P., de Blij, H., 'Geography: Realms, Regions and Concepts'.

7 Uzoige, G., op.cit.

8 Haley, A., 'Roots'.

9 Aldrich, R., 'Greater France: A History of French Overseas Expansion'.

10 Hughes, A,, 'Historical Dictionary of The Gambia.

11 Trimingham, J.S., 'History of Islam in West Africa'.

12 Armstrong, C., 'The Amazingly Graced Life of John Newton', in 'Christianity Today', 2004.

13. Fyfe, C., 'Sierra Leone Inheritance'.

14 Schama, S., 'Rough Crossings'.

15 Fyfe, C., 'A History of Sierra Leone'.

16 Crowther, S.A., 'A Patriot to the Core'; 'Journals'.

17 Bown, D., 'Kingdom People'.

18 Perham, M., 'Lugard'.

19 Bovill, E.W., 'The Golden Trade of the Moors'; 'Caravans of the old Sahara'.

20 Fage, J.D., 'Introduction to The History of West Africa'.

21 Stride, G.T, and Ifeka, C., 'Peoples and Empires in West Africa'.

21 (a) Smith, R.S., 'Warfare and Diplomacy in Pre-Colonial Africa'.

22 Flint, J.E.,'Sir George Goldie and the Making of Modern Nigeria'.

23 Lugard, F., op. cit.

24 Perham, M., op. cit.

25 Bovill, E.W., op.cit.

26 Trimingham, J.S., op. cit.

27 Lugard, F., op.cit.

28 Ademoyega, A.,'The Federation Of Nigeria'.

29 Ologundudu, D., 'The Cradle of Yoruba Culture'

30. Ologundudu, D., op.cit..; Akintoye, S.A. 'A History of The Yoruba People'.

31 Wesley, J., 'The Journal of John Wesley'; Deane, P.A., 'Know Your Methodism'; Sinfield, H.M., 'Methodism's Message in Modern Terms'.

32 Obinyan, V.E., 'Nature of Gods in Edo Ontology'.

33 Aluko, M.E., 'Cultural Wars and National Identity: The Saga Of The Yoruba And The Bini-Edo'.

34 Hernon, A,. 'Britain's Forgotten Wars'.

35 Dark, P., 'An Introduction to Benin Art and Technology Culture'.

36 Akenzua, E.A., 'Oral Tradition of Benin Kingship'.

36a Hogendorn, J., Johnson, M., 'The Shell Money of the Slave Trade'.

37 Akenzua, E.A., op.cit.

37a Equiano, O. (Vasa, G.),' The Interesting Life of Olaudah Equiano'.

38 Ryder, A.F.C., 'Benin and the Europeans, 1485-1897'.

39 Aledeojebi, G., 'History of Yorubaland'.

40 Aledeojebi, A., op.cit.

41 Johnson, S., 'History of Yoruba: From Earliest Time to the beginning of the British Protectorate'.

42 Park, M., 'The Journey of a Mission to The Interior of Africa'; Donahue, J., 'The Exploration Of Africa'.

43 O'Connor, E., 'From The Niger to the Sahara: The Story Of The Archdiocese Of Kaduna'.

44 Smith, M.G., 'Government In Zazzu 1800-1950'; Isaacs, D., 'Nigeria's Emirs: Power behind the Throne'.

45 Trimingham, J.S., op.cit.; Oliver, R., and Fage, J.D., 'A Short History of Africa'; Fage, J.D., 'Introduction to the History of West Africa'.

46 Bosworth, C.E., 'Kano' in 'Historic Cities of The Islamic World'; Trimingham, J.S., op.cit.; Bovill, E.W., op.cit.

47 Bernus, E., 'Les Toureg'; Bourgeot, A., 'Les Societes Touaregues, Nomadisme, Identite, Resistances'.

48 Breunig, P.,'African Sculptutre in Archaeological Contgext; Zangerbadt, L.G., 'History of Jos and Political Development of Nigeria'; Dudley, B.J.,'Politics in Northern Nigeria'.

49 Downes, R.M., 'The Tiv Tribe'.

50 Morris, C., 'Include Me Out'.

51 Matthew VII, 12; Luke VI, 31.

52 Agwu, K., 'Yam and The Igbos'.

53 Isichei, E.A., 'A History of African Societies'.

54 Paton, D., 'Obeah and other Powers: The Politics of Caribbean Healing'.

55 Coleman, J.S., 'Nigeria, Background to Nationalism'.

56 Mwakikagile, G., 'Ethnic Politics in Kenya and Nigeria'.

57 Ezenwa-Ohaeto, E., 'Chinua Achebe: A Biography'.

58 Anene, J.C., 'Southern Nigeria in Transition 1880-1906'.

59 Alpern, S.B., 'Amazons of the Black Sparta'.

60 Law, R., 'Ouidah: The Social History of a West African Slaving Port'.

61 Bay, E.G., 'Wives of The Leopard: Gender, Politics and Culture In The Kingdom of Dahomey'.

62 Pinn, A.B., 'Varieties of African American Religious Experience: Toward a Comprehensive Black Theology'; Metraux, A., 'Voodoo In Haiti'.

63 Bown, D., op. cit.

64 Lawler, N., 'Soldiers, Airmen, Spies and Whisperers: The Gold Coast In World War II'.

65 Lawrence, A.W., 'Trade Castles and Forts of West Africa'.

66 Shaw, E., 'The Quest for Peace and Justice In Liberia'.

67 Pham, J.-P., 'Liberia: Portrait of a Failed State'.

68 Campbell, G., 'Blood Diamonds: Tracing the Deadly Path of the World's Most Precious Stones'.

69 Fernandez-Armesto, F., 'The Canary Islands after the Conquest: The Making of a Colonial Society In the early Sixteenth Century'.

70 Payne, S.G., Palacios, J., 'Franco. A Personal and Political Biography'.

71 Connor, F., 'Liverpool: Our City. Our Heritage'; Olusoga, D., 'A House through Time', Series 1, Episode 1, BBC 2, 2020.

72 Odeyemi, J.O., 'A Political History of Nigeria and the Crisis of Ethnicity in Nation-Building' in I.J.D.S,2014; Eghosa Osaghae, E., 'Crippled Giant: Nigeria Since Independence'.

73 Wordsworth, W., 'On Hearing of the French Revolution'.

74 Denov, M.S., 'Child Soldiers: Sierra Leone's Revolutionary United Front'; Campbell, G., op.cit.

75 Dorman, A.M., 'Blair's Successful War: British Military Intervention In Sierra Leone'.

76 Huband, M., 'The Liberian Civil War'.

77 Hochschild, A., op.cit.

78 Oliver, R. and Fage, J.D., 'A Short History of Africa'.

79 Exodus XVI, 35.

80 Matthew IV, 2.

80 Plato, 'The Republic'.

81 Hick, J., 'God and the Universe of Faiths'.

81a Equiano, O. (Vasa, G.), op.cit.

82 Williams, E., 'Capitalism and Slavery'.

82a July 19th 2020.

82b Afigbo, A.E., 'The abolition of the Slave Trade in Sothern Nigeria, 1185-1950'.

83 John VIII, 1-11.

84 Genesis I, 26.

SELECT BIBLIOGRAPHY

ART, CULTURE & RELIGION (Coast)

Bashole, R., <u>The African Religion of Brazil</u>. Baltimore, 1978.

Clark, P., <u>West Africa and Islam</u>. Edward Arnold, 1982.

Gay, John and Cole, M., <u>The New Mathematics and an Old Culture</u>. Holt, Rinehart& Winston, 1967.

Green, M.M., <u>Ibo Village Affairs</u>. Praeger, 1964.

Harley, G.W., <u>Masks as Agents of Social Control in Northwest Liberia</u>. Peabody.

Herskovits, Melville J. and Frances S., (ed.) <u>Dahomean Narrative: A Cross-Cultural Analysis</u>. Northwestern Univ. Pr, 1998.

Hunwick, John, <u>West Africa, Islam and the Arab World</u>.

Lystad, Robert A., <u>The Ashanti: A Proud People</u>. Rutgers, 1958.

McNaughton, Patrcik R., <u>The Mande Blacksmiths: Knowledge, Power and Art in West Africa</u>. Indiana Univ., 1988.

Rattray, Robert S. <u>Religion & Art in Ashanti</u>. Oxford, 1927.

Sarpong, P. <u>Girls' Nubility Rites In Ashanti</u>. Ghana Publishing Co., 1977.

Schwab, George and Harley, G.W. <u>Tribes of the Liberian Hinterland</u>. Peabody, 1947.

Twumasi, P.A. <u>Medical Systems In Ghana</u>. Ghana Publishing Co., 1975.

Smith, Mary F., <u>Baba of Karo: A Woman of the Muslim Hausa</u>. Yale Univ. Press, 1981.

Senghor, Leopold S., <u>On African Socialism</u>. Praeger, 1961.

Voeks, Robert A, <u>Sacred Leaves of Candomble: African Magic, Medicine, and Religion in Brazil</u> Univ of Texas Pr, 1997.

HISTORY & ECONOMICS (Coast)

Agbodeka, Francis. <u>African Politics & British Policy in the Gold Coast</u>. Longman, 1971.

Apter, David E., <u>Ghana in Transition</u>. Princeton, 1973.

Birmingham, David, <u>Kwame Nkrumah: The Father of African Nationalism</u>. Ohio Univ Press, 1998.

Buah, F.K., <u>A History of Ghana</u>. Macmillian, 1980.

Chatwin, Bruce, <u>Viceroy of Ouidah</u>. Penguin, 1988 (Benin).

Chazan, Naomi H. <u>An Anatomy of Ghanaian Politics</u>. Westview, 1983.

Daaku, Kwame Yeboa, <u>Trade and Politics on the Gold Coast</u>. Oxford, 1970.

Davidson, Basil, <u>A History of West Africa to the Nineteenth Century</u>. Anchor, 1966.

Decalo, Samuel, <u>Historical Dictionary of Benin</u>. Scarecrow, 1976.

Decalo, Samuel, <u>Historical Dictionary of Togo</u>. Scarecrow, 1976.

Equiano, O., <u>Equiano's Travels</u>. Heinemann, 1967 (Abridged edition of the 1789 book.)

Green, Graham, <u>A Journey without Maps</u>. (Sierra Leone & Liberia).

Harrison Church, R.J., <u>West Africa: Environment and Policies</u>. 1976.

Hopkins, A.G., <u>Economic History of West Africa</u>. Longman, 1973.

Levtzion, Nehemia, <u>Medieval West Africa before 1400: Ghana, Takrur, GAO (Songhay) and Mali as Described by Arab Scholars and Merchants</u>. Markus Wiener Pub, 1998. 1-55876-165-9

McFarland, Daniel Miles, <u>Historical Dictionary of Ghana</u>. Scarecrow, 1998.

Price, J.H., <u>Political Institutions of West Africa</u>. Hutchinson, 1975.

Stride, G.T. and Ifeka, C., <u>Peoples and Empires of West Africa</u>. Africana, 1971.

Webster, J.B. and A. Adu Boahen, <u>Revolutionary Years: West Africa Since 1800</u>. Longman, 1967.

Zolberg, Aristide R., <u>One-Party Government in the Ivory Coast</u>. Princeton, 1969.

LITERATURE AND PROVERBS (Coast)

Ariel, Tiny Treasury of African Proverbs.

Bryan, Ashley, <u>The Night Has Ears: African Proverbs</u>. Simon & Schuster Children's, 1999.

De Ley, Gerd, African Proverbs. Hippocrene Books, 1998.

Ibekwe, Patrick, ed. <u>Wit and Wisdom of Africa: Proverbs from Africa and the Caribbean</u>. Africa World Press, 1999.

Achebe, Chinua, <u>A Man of the People</u>. Anchor, 1967. (Nigeria; contemporary urban.)

Achebe, Chinua, <u>Anthills of the Savannah</u>. Heinemann, 1987. (Parable of modern Africa.)

Achebe, Chinua, <u>Arrow of God</u>. (Nigeria; clash between colonial & tradition leader.)

Achebe, Chinua, <u>No Longer at Ease</u>. Heinemann, 1960. (Nigeria; a Western educated man returns and must struggle with forgotten traditional expectations.)

Achebe, Chinua, <u>Things Fall Apart</u>. Fawcett, 1959. (Nigeria; conflicts in a village during the first encounters in the missionary/colonial period.)

Aluko, T.M., <u>One Man, One Matchet</u>. Heinemann, 1964. (Nigeria; a clash between Western science and African politics.)

Aluko, T.M., <u>Kinsman and Foreman</u>. Heinemann, 1966. (Nigeria; after receiving an education, a man finds adjusting to the ways of his village a challenge.)

Amadi, Elechi, <u>The Concubine</u>. Heinemann, 1966. (Nigeria; a woman, romance, values and religion in a traditional Eastern Nigerian society.)

Amadi, Elechi, <u>Great Ponds</u>. Heinemann, 1969. (Nigeria; the feud between two villages is the setting for a story of traditional society in Eastern Nigeria.)

Aniebo, I.N.C., <u>The Journey Within</u>. Heinemann, 1978. (Nigeria; personal struggles in life, confused with traditional and Christian values.)

Armah, Ayi Kewi, <u>The Beautyful Ones Are Not Yet Born</u>. Heinemann, 1969. (Ghana; a powerful portrayal of the power of corruption.)

Badian, Seydou, translated by Marie-Terese Noiset, <u>Caught in the Storm</u>. Lynne Rienner Pub., 1998.

Bowen, Elenore Smith, <u>Return to Laughter</u>. Anchor, 1964. (Nigeria; a Western woman observes the women of a traditional village.)

Conteh, Osman, <u>Unanswered Cries</u>. Macmillan, 2002. (Sierra Leone (Temne); a young girl challenges the Bondo Society and ritual for female genital cutting.)

Djoleto, Amu, <u>The Strange Man</u>. Heinemann, 1968. (Ghana; a boy growing-up, schools, corruption and reconciling a man's role in his family.)

Djoleto, Amu, <u>Money Galore</u>. Heinemann, 1975. (Ghana; post-independence politics, corruption, scandals and tragedy.)

Echewa, T. Obinkaram, <u>I Saw the Sky Catch Fire</u>. Dutton, 1992. (Historical fiction about women in Nigeria.)

Gay, John, <u>Red Dust on the Green Leaves</u>. InterCultural Assoc., 1973. (Liberia; one brother follows traditional ways while the other brother goes away to school.)

Herbstein, Manu, <u>Ama: A Story of the Atlantic Slave Trade</u>. e-reads Publications, 2001. (Historical fiction: Story told by an African girl who is kidnapped into slavery. It is set on the Slave Coast of West Africa (Senegal to Ghana) and in Brazil. An excellent but at times very grim story.)

Iroh, Eddie, <u>Forty-Eight Guns for the General</u>. Heinemann, 1976. (Nigeria; set during the Biafra War, the novel critically examines mercenaries.)

Iroh, Eddie, <u>Toads of War</u>. Heinemann, 1979. (Nigeria; set during the Biafra War, the novel critically examines those who live well and get rich off of war.)

Iroh, Eddie, <u>The Siren In The Night</u>. Heinemann, 1982. (Nigeria; a thriller set after the Biafra War when not all the scores are settled.)

Knebel, Fletcher, <u>The Zinzin Road</u>. Doubleday, 1966. (A development worker's idealism clashes with politics and corruption in a country resembling Liberia.)

Laye, Camara, <u>The Dark Child</u>. Noonday, 1954. (Guinea; observations of a boy.)

Laye, Camara, <u>The Radiance of the King</u>. Fontana, 1965. (Guinea.)

Munonye, John, <u>Obi</u>. Heinemann, 1969. (Nigeria; Traditional values come in conflict with a couple's Christian learning when they return to the village.)

Munonye, John, <u>Oil Man of Obange</u>. Heinemann, 1971. (Nigeria; a brother & sister endure hardship to get an education.)

Nwankwo, N., <u>Danda</u>. Heinemann, 1964. (A ne'er-do-well clashes with his father.)

Nwapa, Flora, <u>Efuru</u>. Heinemann, 1966. (Nigeria; A story of a strong woman, a village, and traditional values and beliefs.)

Nwapa, Flora, <u>Idu</u>. Heinemann, 1970. (Nigeria; A woman's life demonstrates traditional values for children, husbands, death and life.)

Nzekwu, Onuora, <u>Blade among the Boys</u>. Heinemann, 1962. (Nigeria; the conflicts between the religion of a man's ancestors and Roman Catholicism.)

Okri, Ben, <u>The Famished Road</u>. Doubleday, 1993. (This book illustrates the movement between the "This World and the "Other World." If you are having trouble following this it may help to read pages 487-8, or to read Malidoma Patrice Somé's <u>Healing Wisdom of Africa: Finding Life Purpose through Nature, Ritual and Community</u>. Okri is kind of an African Gabriel Garcia Marquez. He can be a little heady for the uninitiated.)

Peters, Lenrie, <u>Second Round</u>. Heinemann, 1965. (Sierra Leone; A doctor's troubled and unsatisfying life in Freetown.)

Selormey, Francis, <u>The Narrow Path</u>. Heinemann, 1966. (Ghana; a boy's life in fishing village, describing customs and family relationships.)

Soyinka, Wole, <u>The Interpreters</u>. Collier, 1965. (Nigeria; hopes, loves, and hates, among the new intellectuals.)

Tutuola, Amos, <u>Palm-Wine Drinkard and My Life in the Bush of Ghosts</u>.

Umeasiegbu, Rems Nna, <u>The Way We Lived</u>. Heinemann, 1969. (Nigeria; stories of the customs and cultures of a people in Eastern Nigeria.)

Warner, Esther, <u>New Song in a Strange Land</u> (1948), <u>The Crossing Fee</u> and <u>Seven Days To Lomaland</u>. Houghton Mifflin. (Several books by the author's, adventure in traditional West Africa.)

WEST AFRICA: Sahel
ART, CULTURE & RELIGION (Sahel)

"Mali's Dogon People" National Geographic, Oct 1990.

Beckwith, Carol, <u>Nomads of Niger</u>. Abrams, 1993.

Briggs, Lloyd Cabot, <u>Living Races of the Sahara Desert</u>. Harvard U, 1958.

Briggs, Lloyd Cabot, <u>Tribes of the Sahara</u>. Harvard U, 1960.

Englebert, V. "Drought Threatens the Tuareg World", National Geographic, Apr 1974.

Fisher, Allen G. and Fisher Humphrey J., <u>Slavery and Muslim Society in Africa: The Institution in Saharan and Sudanic Africa</u>. Markus Wiener Pub, 2000.

Gerster, Georg, "River of Sorrow, River of Hope", National Geographic, Aug 1975.

Gerster, Georg, <u>Sahara: Desert of Destiny</u>. Ayer Co Pub., 1970.

Skinner, Elliott P., <u>Mossi of the Upper Volta: The Political Development of a Sudanese People</u>. Stanford U, 1964.

Somé, Malidoma Patrice, <u>Of Water and the Spirit: Ritual, Magic, and Initiation in the Life of an African Shaman</u>. Penguin, 1995.

HISTORY & ECONOMICS (Sahel)

"Jenne-Jeno, West Africa's Oldest City", National Geographic, Sept 1982

Baier, S. <u>Economic History of Central Niger</u>. Clarendon, 1980.

Barth, Heinrich, <u>Travels and Discoveries in North and Central Africa</u>. London, 1965.

Bovill, Edward W., <u>The Golden Trade of the Moors: West African Kingdoms in the Fourteenth Century</u>. Markus Wiener Pub, 1998.

Bovill, Edward W. <u>The Niger Explored</u>. London, 1968.

Cabral, Amilcar, <u>Revolution in Guinea: Selected Texts</u>. Stage 1, 1969.

Clarke, Thurston. <u>Last Caravan</u>. Putnam and Sons, 1978.

Corbett, Edward M., <u>The French Presence In Black Africa</u>. Black Orpheus, 1971.

Courlander, Harold and Sako, Ousmane. The Heart of the Ngoni: Heroes of the African Kingdom of Segu. Crown, 1982. (Kingdom of Segu.)

Curtain, Philip. Rise and Fall of the Plantation Complex: Essays in Atlantic History. Cambridge Univ Press, 1990 (Re: Atlantic slave trade.)

Decalo, Samuel, Historical Dictionary of Niger. Scarecrow, 1976.

DeGramont, Sanche, Strong Brown God: The Story of the Niger River. Houghton Mifflin, Boston 1976. (Account of the exploration & opening of the fabled West African river, that was resisted as much by the Africans as it was by the mosquitoes.)

Djata, Sundiata A.K., The Bamana Empire By the Niger: Kingdom, Jihad and Colonialization, 1712-1920. Markus Wiener Pub, 1998.

Glatz, M.H., Politics of Natural Disaster: The Case of the Sahel Drought. Greenwood Pub., 1976.

Gwin, Peter, "Lost Tribes of the Green Sahara", National Geographic, Sept 2008.

Hammer, Joshua, The Bad-Ass Librarian of Timbuktu. Simon & Schuster, 2016.

Hargreaves, John D., West Africa: The Former French States. Prentice-Hall, 1967.

Imperato, Pascal James, Historical Dictionary of Mali. Scarecrow, 1977.

Lupton, Kenneth. Mungo Park: The African Traveler. Oxford, 1976.

McFarland, Daniel Miles, Historical Dictionary of Burkina Faso. Scarecrow, 1998.

Moulton, Jeanne M., Animation Rurale: Education for Rural Development. Center for International Education, U of Massachusetts, 1977.

Nachtigal, Gustav and Fisher, Allan G., Sahara and Sudan: Bornu, Kanem, Borku, Ennedi. London, 1971.

Oloruntimehin, B.O., Segu Tukulor Empire. Humanities Pr, 1972.

Villiers, Marq & Hirtle, Sheila, Into Africa: A Journey Through the Ancient Empires. Key Porter Books, 1997.

Welch, Galbraith, Unveiling of Timbuctoo. Carroll and Graf, New York 1991 - orig. pub. 1939 by William Morrow, NY. This is a wonderfully riveting account account of Caillié's explorations and eventual journey to and from Timbuktu.

MODERN LITERATURE (Sahel)

Ba, Miriama, So Long a Letter. New Horn, 1981. (Senegal; reflections on tradition by a Moslem woman.)

Conde, Maryse, Segu. Ballantine Books, 1987. (Mali; historical fiction. Very readable and covers a lot of 18th and 19th century West African history.)

Ekwensi, Cyprian O., Burning Grass. Longman, 1962. (Nigeria; pride of a woman herder.)

Niane, D.T., Sundiata: An Epic of Old Mali. Longman, 1965. (Guinea; a story transcribed from a traditional griot.)

Ousmane, Sembene, God's Bits of Wood. Heinemann, 1962. (Senegal & Mali; The gripping lives of the people in the 1947-8 Dakar-Niger railway workers strike.)

Ousmane, Sembene, Money-Order with White Genesis. Heinemann, 1987.

Ousmane, Sembene, Xala. Heinemann, 1990.

Ousmane, Sembene, <u>Last of the Empire</u>. Heinemann, 1984.Ousmane, Sembene, Selected filmography: Borom Sarret (1963), Niaye (1964), La Noire de … (1966), Mandabi (1968), Xala (1974), Ceddo (1977), Camp de Thiaroye (1988), Guelwaar (1992), Faat Kiné (2000), and Moolaadé (2004),

NATURAL HISTORY

Serle, W., Morel, Gerald J. & Hartwig, W. <u>Collins Field Guide: Birds of West Africa</u>. Collins, 1997

Swift, Jeremy. <u>Sahara</u> . Time-Life, 1975.

INDEX

Printed and bound by CPI Group (UK) Ltd, Croydon, CR0 4YY